I DIDN'T PLAN FOR THIS BUT GOD DID

JALIA WALLACE

We humans keep brainstorming options and plans,
but God's purpose prevails.

PROVERBS 19:21

ISBN: 978-1-7349439-4-8 Library of Congress Cataloging-in-Publication Date is available.

Project Specialist/Author Coach
Barlow Enterprises, LLC
Write Your Book Now! Visit: www.destinystatement.com or Text
478-227-5692

Legal Disclaimer

While none of the stories in this book are fabricated, some of the names and details may have been changed to protect the privacy of the individuals mentioned. Although the author and publisher have made every effort to ensure that the information in this book was correct at time of press, the author and publisher do not assume and hereby disclaim any liability to any party for any loss, damage, or disruption caused by errors or omissions, whether such errors or omissions result from negligence, accident, or any other cause.

Ordering Information

I Didn't Plan for This may be purchased in large quantities at a discount for educational, business, or sales promotional use. For more information or to request Ms. Jalia Wallace as the speaker at your next event email: jaliaswallace@gmail.com.

To my grandparents, who I never got the chance to meet physically, but who have been with me all along in spirit. I love you and I will meet you in heaven.

Howard Francis Wallace Jr.

Joan Claudette Wallace

To my first cousin, better known as the best big-brother I never had. I lost you the day after my twenty-second birthday. I will love you forever.

Darrell Antwon Wallace

To my one and only Godchild, who I love very much. You motivate me to push harder.

Drue Achilles Barnes

and uncovered more than I anticipated. Knowing her, I assumed much of what she would say would be things I already knew or that we have discussed in our many long talks, but I was pleasantly surprised. She reveals and shares things she's dealt with and is dealing with, in a way that brings healing to the reader. Her transparency makes for an easy read and allows the reader to relate to her directly. It is less of a read and more of an experience.

Jalia takes you along with her, journeying through struggles of the past and offering clarity on how she made it through. Her honesty is admirable and sparks a fire within me as a reader to persevere. We don't always plan for the curve balls life throws us, but it is up to us to take a swing. Jalia's story inspires hope and is uplifting. This book aids those who are in a place of uncertainty with direct references to the Bible and with advice about the specific things that we all battling with. This book is not meant to coddle but to encourage, and it does just that.

DE'SHON GREEN
ACTRESS/EVENT COORDINATOR

Are you ready to go on an inspirational journey? Well, this is that book! Be prepared for moments when you'll laugh, moments of tears, and you may even find yourself shouting out loud. OKAY! There are so many takeaways and strategies for moving forward throughout the book. I am grateful to have taken this journey, Lee-Lee thanks for being transparent and Unapologetically You! I am reminded of the late great Albertina Walker gospel classic. It speaks volumes and relates to what I have read and been reminded of from reading your book: "Please be patient with me, God's not through with me yet. When God gets through with me, I will come forth . . . I will come forth as pure gold!"

ELIZABETH PETTUS
CREATING SUSTAINABILITY & INNOVATION
CONSULTANT/CEO

An exceptional and fantastic read! Jalia really displays her individuality as she tells her story and throughout her book, there are moments of hilarity, inspiration, and expression! I Didn't Plan for This *is a must-read!*

WARREN COLEMAN
AUTHOR/UNCONVENTIONAL LEADER

We all need to be more transparent when it comes down to how we try to plan our lives. We try to plan what career path we will take, when we will be married, and how life's supposed to be. We plan, but sometimes, our plans unexpectedly fail and our worlds are turned upside down — but with God, we still come out on top!

If you have had to deal with sudden, hard changes to your life plans this is the book for you! Jalia shares personal stories that many aren't willing to tell. The way she shares helps us to reflect on our mistakes and reminds us that life is a constant journey. Jalia also reminds us that although life may not go as planned, God has something so much greater in store when we place him in the center of our plan. God will take the unqualified and transform them. When we seek our purpose we will encounter roadblocks that can deter us from following God's plan, but with God's help, we can overcome any situation.

Thank you, Jalia for putting your story into words to remind us that God's love, grace, guidance, and mercy will turn what wasn't planned into a masterpiece.

BRELYN WILLIAMS
CORPORATE EXECUTIVE

CONTENTS

Introduction

It is important to me that I begin my conversation with you with a confession. At one time, I used to believe that all of the people who authored books wrote because they had overcome something. I imagined that these authors were in their best states of mind and well-being or that the person who had written and had their book published had accomplished something truly exceptional. While some of what I imagined as the prerequisites or qualifications for authoring a book are definitely true, being a first-time author has caused me to completely rethink my prior assumptions. Having written and published a book of my own now, I realize that the pressure I put on authors to have accomplished amazing things or to have overcome incredible odds of some sort, are not even required to write and share something significant and useful with the world. While that is sometimes the case, it is not always true.

Along those lines, instead of blindsiding you, I want to tell you where I stand as an author. More specifically, as a first-time author, I write while still figuring it all out. I am writing, while I am still going through the process. I want you to be encouraged by this book. However, I do not want you to look at this like every other book. Instead, I want you to truly imagine that you and I are in a room conversing with one another. In essence, I want you to know that I am extending my hand and heart to you and saying, "Let's go through this process together."

Picture this: Life is all figured out. Everything is going as planned. In fact, things are better than you could have ever imagined. You're getting ten thousand or more likes on your Instagram pictures. Jesus just friended you on Facebook. Chick fil A is open on Sunday, and you are totally and completely living your life on purpose. You're just unapologetically killing the game. Literally nothing is going wrong. I know you're probably laughing at this, but this is really what most people would call the best life.

Next, imagine showing up to gym class in grade school and being improperly dressed, being pulled over by a cop and not having your driver's license or car registration with you, or even arriving to a class to take a test, then realizing that you have nothing to write with. Preparation is important, isn't it? When it comes to being prepared, it always seems that the more prepared we are, the better off we are. I like to imagine that life is smooth sailing, when we are prepared. A "smooth sailing" life is the kind of life we plan for, when we are younger. In our childlike minds, we expect that as long as we are prepared, we will experience something like "The Best Life."

I'm, therefore, about to admit something that I'd usually never want to admit, even if someone called me out on it. Well, ummmmm, that's the fact I am a control freak. Yes, I said it! I want to control everything. I don't know why I hesitate to admit it, because I know that a lot of us want to be in control. Of course, some people want control more than others, but the need to feel somewhat in charge of things is not abnormal. People want to be in control. They at least want to feel like they are in control.

We all know in life there are several things that, especially in the early stages of our lives, we prepare for prematurely (well at least we try to). For instance, before we even have a clue about who we will marry, we prepare for how we want our wedding to be, how many children we will have, when we will finish school, what career path we'll choose, the purchase of our dream house and more. Consequently, there are also a host of life events that we do not quite prepare as much for, if we prepare for them at all. These are the things that we say, "just happen" in life. These events include inescapable instances like death, failure, generational curses, insecurity, etc. I could go on forever listing the many unplanned things that happen in our lives. However, since you're human like I am, you get the point.

When you hear the word creative, what comes to mind? Many people only associate the word creative with art. However, creativity extends into many more aspects of our lives than art. Creative people think very far outside the box. They usually see things much more deeply than those who are less creative, because of the way they think. While the majority of people look solely at the surface, creative people look at the bigger picture. While most people only look at the opportunities that are placed in front of them, creative people look to create opportunities to set before themselves and others. Creative people never stop thinking and they never really go with the flow of things. On the contrary, creatives create the flow. Now, that's me! After all of their planning and after all of their preparing, what's a creative-minded person to do, when their plans continuously fail? What do they do? Needless to say, growing up, I was a different kind of child. Not only was I different, I was very creative. I wanted to dress creatively, think creatively, use my time creatively and even respond to situations creatively. I was never normal. I became aware that I was different at a young age. Weird? I know. I mean I could probably say that my creative juices started flowing at an early age.

I always knew that I was an outcast, but I just never knew why. I was born with a vivid imagination and I had a strong desire to make an impact on the world. I had a strong sense of self as a child. I believe that, after a certain point in my life, my parents just knew that regardless of whether they told me yes or no, I was always going to pave my own way. If they didn't give me an answer, I'd eventually come up with one. I had to have been a very annoying kid. I always wanted to be in control. I bet they love me even more for this character trait now (at least I hope they do). I was a very, very persistent kid, who wanted to do a bunch of things and who never wanted to be told, "No." I was a handful. I'd go from building things out of whatever I could get my hands on, to playing until I won every possible video game I owned, to running little businesses with my cousins and sisters (lemonade stand chronicles), to playing a violin, to choreographing dances with my cousins and friends, to putting together presentations, to building tree houses, to turning cardboard boxes into cars and much more. No matter what my next adventure was, I always did one thing first. I was always strategic. I would not be found unprepared. I always planned first. I would plan, and I would plan and I would plan some more. I planned for everything.

I instinctively knew how to strategically plan things out and then take the steps necessary to carry out that plan. Even when I was young, I had usually clear, vivid visions in my head of the way I wanted certain events to play out. Even if, in fact, what I'd imagined ended up being a complete catastrophe, it was never because of my lack of planning and preparing.

I was a very imaginative kid living in my own uniquely crafted, imaginary world. My cousins and I planned shows that we'd perform at family gatherings. I'm pretty sure you did too, but we took our practices very seriously. For some reason, I feel like whenever I didn't really plan for something, I ended up making really impulsive decisions. I remember when I first told my dad that I wanted a new car (which is the car I have now). He told me I should wait and just finish paying off the car that I had (considering it was almost paid off), so I could just be without a car payment. I told him that I really wanted another car. He knew that it would have been the best decision for me to not get the car, which is why he tried to convince me not to. While I did not get it that same day, unfortunately, within the next week or two, I went to the dealership and got the car. This is a perfect example of my willful personality. I guess you can also say that my decision not to plan and prepare for how I would purchase my next car, resulted in my making an impulsive decision. With the car scenario, I'd created such a strong vision of myself in the car I wanted that, despite I wanted and did not need a new car, I'd convinced myself I *needed* that car.

When I was cheerleader, it took practice after practice for my team to perfect our routine to the degree that we were ready to perform at competitions. It took a lot of practicing and preparing, before we hit the stage. Otherwise, we would be up there making fools of ourselves and if we did not practice, we would not have ended up in first, second, third, fourth, or even fifth place. When I played the violin, we had school concerts about twice a year. Although we only performed twice a year, we spent every day in school preparing for those two concerts. Don't get me wrong. What we plan and prepare for is not always just about the big performances. I recall having mini pep talks with myself, before asking my parents what I felt like was a serious question. My sister and I would literally plan everything out, whenever we were about to ask my parents for something. As much as I prepared my team, my fellow musicians and my sister for our presentations, I did not only prepare for the task with the people I worked with. I was also sure to spend considerable time preparing the person who mattered most in all of these situations. I knew I was the only person I could genuinely control and that if I didn't prepare myself properly, I would only have one person to blame — ME.

When we experience moments in our lives that result from our failure to prepare, we are usually disappointed. The hardest person to blame is ourselves. We often want to point the finger away from ourselves.

We never want "it" to be our fault, no matter what that "it" is. We always want more than we prepare for. We want the reaping without sowing. We want success without time. We want joy without pain. We want life without God. The key word here is "want." A little secret I've learned, is that you cannot get what you want without true preparation. Believe it or not, true preparation cannot begin with anyone other than you. Yes, getting help is nice. Help is valuable. However, it all starts with YOU. Are you really preparing for what you want? Are you really preparing yourself so that when you get what you want or, what you believe you want, you'll be ready to handle and steward it?

Have you ever found yourself questioning your self-worth? Have you ever questioned your abilities? Have you questioned your purpose altogether? If you've answered no, I am confident that you are telling a white lie to avoid hurting your own feelings. Jesus even questioned His purpose. He asked if the reason He entered the world, to bear our sins upon the cross and redeem the world, could be taken from him. Notice that I did not say He gave up or that He did not fulfill His calling. However, he did question it. And guess what? He didn't plan for that. We all want to believe that we were put on earth for a reason, but just what might that reason be? You may be here for several reasons, but you will never fully know until you truly work to discover and then prepare for our purpose in life.

When I reflected on everything that I have ever prepared for, I came to grips with the fact there is one thing I never adequately got ready for. I had never prepared to be my best self, when I had to deal with things for which I had not planned. I was not good at dealing with the unknown. However, I have come to respect and realize that some of the most important training that we can undergo is training that equips us to be the best version of ourselves, when we are forced to deal with life events for which we were not prepared.

We all face challenges every day. Some of these challenges are so serious that they have the potential to hinder us from believing we can get better. This is precisely why, becoming your best self requires that we work on both our internal and external realities. You must not only acknowledge, examine and fix what is happening inside of you, but you must do the same when it comes to how you react.

Remember, our thoughts are just as important as our words. In fact, thinking something can be more powerful, because what you think will influence what you believe and ultimately, what you do. The Bible reminds us that even our thoughts can be sinful.

Preparing to be your best self is hard work. A lot of healing must happen during this time. Arriving at our best self is definitely not an overnight process. On the contrary, this level of personal development is something that you will work at for the rest of your life. There will always be new ways to improve yourself. This is one of the reasons why I do not believe that you have to be a perfect person (no one is) to be good, or at least better, than you were, as time progresses. Once you decide to develop yourself from within, the more you will flourish. Changes from within always show up on the outside.

Now let me ruffle your feathers a little. You do know that no matter how much you prepare for things, there are times when everything you've planned and prepared for will fall apart? I mean completely fall apart. No seriously, there are times when nothing you've prepared for will happen and when everything you prepared for won't. However, guess what? You know what else you must learn through the process?

You must learn to trust God.

Believe me, it's much easier said than done but you will get there. This book is your mini guide to help you deal with your unexpected, *"I didn't plan for this"* kind of moments. I don't know about you, but I have these kinds of moments on a regular basis. Let's overcome our challenges and difficulties, while staying encouraged, stepping over challenges, learning to trust God and becoming who God called us to be.

Jalia

Part I:

UNPREPARED

Chapter 1

PLAN TO BE UNPREPARED

UNPLANNED AND BEAUTIFUL

When we are younger, we tend to believe that life is a beautiful thing. Don't misunderstand me, "Life *is* definitely an AMAZING thing." However, you and I both know that it's not always peaches and cream. Picture life without hurt, pain and disappointments. Imagine life without anything other than what is good. For those who had happy childhoods, the amazing moments of our lives are what define how we see life. When we are young, we really tend to think that life has no disappointments or pain. We seldom consider the bad times we will experience or encounter in our lives. However, as we grow older and we start to experience tragedy and other unfortunate circumstances, we learn to cope along the way.

I remember my first friend. His name was Noah. He was a Caucasian boy, who was about a year or two younger than I was. Noah and I did literally everything together. We ate lunch and dinner together, dressed up in superhero costumes together (yes,

I was that kid), played video games, climbed trees, rode bikes, played in the dirt and whatever else we could, as we played and had fun together. Noah and I were adventurous. I never paid attention to the difference in our skin color. I just knew that when I was around Noah, I could be myself. Sometimes, I was more myself with him, than I was with some of my girlfriends. I never felt like I had to prove anything to him. We didn't like each other as anything more than friends. We were very young but we were interested in the same exact things. I believe we started to hang out, when we were about four or five years old. You may think, "Wow, that's young." However, my parents had no problem letting me be a kid. As long as I was in the house at the time that they said to be, and they knew where I was. My friend's parents had spoken with mine, so there were no issues. I forgot to tell you that Noah lived next door to us. Although we were different in a number of ways, I never questioned our connection or why I was such good friends with him. This is the beauty of being a child. Children don't focus as much on the differences of the people around them, as adults tend to. Instead, they just go with the flow and enjoy being with whoever they are with. I never planned to be Noah's friend. It just happened. It was just a beautiful experience that wasn't planned. Talk about a beautiful unplanned moment in life, right? There was nothing to be afraid of and nothing to complain about. There was no tragedy and no pain. Just Noah, happiness, and me.

UNPLANNED AND UGLY

Let me now share a few times in my life for which I did not prepare. I'll just tell you now that the outcomes were not great.

In my sophomore year of high school (I remember it like it was yesterday), anyone would tell you that I was one of the friendliest people you'd meet. You could never tell when I was having a bad day. I was always laughing, making jokes, smiling, helping people, cheering people up and just talking to everyone—even people I didn't know.

In the beginning of my sophomore year (in 2009), I completely and suddenly changed. I literally lost myself. Losing yourself can put you into a very deep depression. Unless you have experienced this, it is difficult to imagine how low you can sink into sadness, when you just don't feel like yourself anymore. Suddenly and without warning, I became overwhelmed with feelings and thoughts that I was doing everything wrong. I did not want to get out of bed and go to school (or go anywhere for that matter). I had the worst thoughts in my head. I stopped eating. I cried more than I did anything else. I also spoke the worst affirmations over myself. I was not sure who this person I was becoming was, but I knew she was not who I wanted to be. Was it a mid-teen crisis? I never thought I would have suicidal thoughts, but when you're this depressed, you think of reasons not to live rather than for reasons to be here.

I felt like I had a huge dark cloud over me. I was constantly asking myself "what if" questions about my existence. It was just very peculiar, because I was really the girl who everyone always counted on to cheer them up. However, for some reason, I suddenly felt like I had no one I could turn to. This is not to say that I didn't have good friends, but I just completely shut down. I was already a Christian at that time in my life. Unfortunately, I was so sad that I didn't believe that prayer or God were options that could help me. I was the saddest I had ever been, and I really couldn't put my finger on exactly why. What made it worse, is that I still appeared to be my happy go lucky self, but deep inside I was fighting a constant battle. It felt like I was battling myself and losing the battle every single day.

I went on like that for months, until one day, I completely broke down. I just couldn't take feeling that way anymore, so I went to the counseling center in my high school It was an area where students could go when they were upset or sad and just wanted to vent, adjust, or find ways to cope. The center was a set of separate offices on the other side of the school. I only went because I knew that I couldn't handle being in class without crying. I started to talk to a woman there . I talked to her at school. Eventually, she had a therapist come to my house a few days each week to talk with me at home. Unfortunately, I didn't truly want to talk to them, so I would not open up. I honestly only said things that would get them out of my face. Consequently, I was not getting to the core of my issues. Since I refused to be around people during this time, I spent much more time by myself than ever before. While it was terribly difficult for me, I think that spending time alone largely contributed to my ability to find myself again. It took time and preparation. However, slowly but surely, I regained my composure and eventually, I went from being a complete wreck to being happy again. I hardly remember how I got through it all, but I can tell you that I did. I had to prepare to find myself again. I had also to prepare myself to be genuinely happy again. It needed to be real from the inside and not just fake from the outside. I had to focus more on who I was, rather than who I wasn't. While I do not recall every detail of how I recovered, I do remember constantly speaking positive affirmations over my life.

I never planned, at 15 years of age, to suddenly and without clear cause become the saddest I had ever been in my life, lose myself and battle suicidal thoughts. I didn't prepare for any of that. I could not have prepared. However, I did survive it and I came out of the experience stronger and wiser than before. We have to realize that even though we want to prepare for everything, sometimes things like that just happen without any warning and without giving you an opportunity to prepare. I wasn't given any warning signs.

Something terrible doesn't always have to happen for you to lose yourself. Losing yourself is something that all of us experience at some point in our lives. I'm not saying that everyone will go through depression. However, at some point, if it hasn't already happened, you will lose yourself. Just keep on living and remember this: You have to prepare to be unprepared.

One of the hardest things about depression, is that you will stay depressed not because you just don't want to be receptive. It is because most of the time you have no idea why you are depressed. You just know that you don't want to feel anymore. It feels like you're drowning and you're not even in water. Nevertheless, sometimes on the road to preparing to become your best self, you will lose yourself. In my case, I "had" to lose myself to find myself.

Plan to be Unprepared

When we are younger, we tend to believe that life is a beautiful thing. Don't misunderstand me, "Life *is* definitely an AMAZING thing." However, you and I both know that it's not always peaches and cream.

> *For everything there is a season, A time for every activity under heaven.*
>
> ECCLESIASTES 3:1-8

REFLECTION QUESTIONS

1. Take yourself back to a time when something in your life occurred that was very unplanned but ended up being a very beautiful moment. Reminisce on how it made you feel. What made the moment so beautiful?

____

____

____

____

2. Take yourself back to a time when something in your life occurred that was very unplanned and ended up being a very ugly moment. Reminisce on how it made you feel. Was it something that you believe could have been avoided? If so, how could it have been avoided? What were your reactions? Reflect on how it may have changed you or your perspective.

____

____

____

____

Chapter 2

EMBRACE FAILURE

CULTURE DEFINES SUCCESS

At some point, we all look at successful people and think to ourselves, "I want to be like them." We find ourselves craving the success that they have and the life they live. However, in the process of yearning for what they have attained, we forget to consider the roadblocks and failures they had to endure on the path to their success. Whether we want to believe it or not, every successful person has failed far more than once. In fact, most have failed hundreds, if not thousands, of times. The power behind a successful person is not that they are good at "not failing." On the contrary, their power lies in the fact that they know how to embrace their failures and move forward.

We all experience failure. How we respond when we fail is very important, because our response determines our next steps. It also affects how much farther towards accomplishing our goals we will be able to go.

Let's consider examples of the successful people around us today. A few examples of some inspirational, successful people who have failed are Bill Gates, Walt Disney and Oprah Winfrey. They all are very successful now. However, they have also failed a lot, just like you and me.

Bill Gates who, according to an April 2020 survey by *Forbes*, is the second richest man in the world. His current net worth is 104 billion dollars. He is known as the man who built Microsoft, the largest software company in the world. However, did you know that Bill Gates failed before he succeeded?

When he was seventeen years old, Bill and his friend Paul Allen, who was only nineteen years old, started a business called Traf-O-Data. This business failed completely but Bill Gates kept thinking, working and pursuing new ideas. Can you imagine if he had given up after his first failed business? We may never know the answer to that question, but we do know that he definitely would not be one of the richest men in the world.

Gates went on to attend the top ranked business school in the world, Harvard Business School. Gaining admission into Harvard is not easy. Even a 4.0 GPA is not enough to get into that school. In 1975, two years into his studies, Gates dropped out of Harvard Business School to start his business, Microsoft, with his friend, Paul Allen. Can you imagine dropping out of a top-ranked university to start a business that could easily fail, just like his first business failed? Can you picture the disappointment he felt from failing the first time and the nervousness he felt from getting ready to try again?

Ultimately, he believed he could be a driving force in the software industry. Despite failing, his vision and drive remained relentless. Let's be real, I can be disappointed to the point of giving up, when I fail a test that I studied hard for. Yet, he did not drown in his failure, he embraced it. He took everything he learned from starting his first business and applied it to starting Microsoft. He ended up becoming one of the most successful and wealthiest businessmen in the world.

Walt Disney, who is known for creating the best childhood experience for every single person who is reading this, also experienced failure. Disney was an American entrepreneur, animator, voice actor and film producer. If you get the picture of Disney World in your head, that is Walt. Walt was actually fired as a newspaper editor, because he was told that he lacked imagination and good ideas. OUCH! That was an unwanted, unplanned gift of failure and rejection all wrapped up into one. He was told that he was not good enough for exactly what he was destined to accomplish—using his imagination to make children happy. That was Walt Disney's mission. Did Walt Disney listen to that newspaper editor? He may have at first, but he did not let that editor's comments stop him from moving forward. Like Gates, Disney had started a number of businesses that did not last long. He even ended up having to declare bankruptcy! Nonetheless, instead of giving up, just like Bill Gates, Walt Disney kept pressing along. Eventually, he found extraordinary success.

Now, let's talk about Oprah Winfrey! She is world renowned for "The Oprah Winfrey Show." She is an American media executive, actress, talk show host, television producer and philanthropist. Oprah is one of those people I often look at and just say, "WOW!" How can one black woman be so successful? Oprah faced a very hard road to get where she is.

She survived a very difficult and abusive childhood and numerous career setbacks, including being told she was unfit for television. Again, like Gates and Disney, Oprah kept working, despite all of the hardships and failures she endured. She became one of the most successful black women in the world.

SUCCESS REDEFINED BY PURPOSE

I know that all of the people that I just mentioned are, by societal standards, phenomenally successful. However, success is not one dimensional. I define success in terms of whether a person is walking in their purpose. This is not to say that Gates, Disney and Oprah are not walking in their purposes. The fact that they were so passionate and refused to let failures stop them actually indicates that they were working with and for a greater purpose. Years ago, when I was much less mature, I defined a person's success based on how much money they had, the type of work they were doing and their lifestyle. However, my mindset has changed.

I now define success by whether a person consults God, seeks their calling and follows their purpose. My pastor, Dharius Daniels, for example, is a truly successful person. His story amazed me as soon as I heard it. He was attending law school, when God pretty much interrupted his plans and he became a preacher. I don't think you should underestimate or take the need to quickly change course lightly either. Imagine working hard going to school for something you really have a passion for and then BOOM! God calls you to something else. He is now literally one of the greatest communicators and pastors in the world. However, he had no idea that this is where

God would lead him. He was just obedient and he followed his purpose.

I really used to want the type of success celebrated by mainstream culture. However, as I grow in my relationship with God, I want nothing more than to leave this earth knowing that I fulfilled His purpose for my life.

There is one other person that I would like to mention who embraced tremendous difficulty more than any other person. His name is Jesus Christ. Jesus was a perfect man but He had to endure hardships we could never even fathom going through.

Let's consider Adam and Eve. When God put Adam and Eve in the Garden of Eden, he gave them simple instructions and they failed. It's not that they didn't know what to do. It's not that they had no choice but to do the wrong thing. They did the wrong thing because they only considered what they wanted at that moment. They did not think about the consequences. Of course, looking back, we all say we don't understand why they couldn't just have made the right decision. However, doesn't this sound just like most of us? We sometimes make mistakes in the heat of the moment, ignoring instructions given and then look back at how things could have played out, if we would had done things differently. We then have to deal with the failure. Well, of course, for them, that one mistake changed a lot. It didn't just affect Adam and Eve. It affected the whole world. Some mistakes we make do not only affect our lives, but they affect the lives of those around us. Embracing failure is definitely possible, but that doesn't mean you should purposely make mistakes that could have been completely avoided. After the mistake Adam and Eve made, there was no turning back. The consequence of their decision was that we were all born into a world of sin. Thankfully, our heavenly father had grace and did something that would still allow us to live with him eternally. Thankfully, God decided to send his son Jesus Christ to die for our sins, to wash them all away and to give us a chance to live eternal life with him despite what Adam and Eve did. This is a prime example of how God embraces failure. He could have just focused on the fact that they messed up and let us live in sin. He did not have to give us another chance, but He did. Let's think logically: Can you imagine giving up your only child to die for other people's wrongdoings? We barely like to pay for our own mistakes, so imagine having to pay for someone else's? Imagine having to pay with your child's life? I don't know about you, but the thought of it is just wildly absurd. Maybe that's why they call Him the great and powerful God, because He surely did it.

Now let's think about Jesus's time on the cross. If you've ever seen *The Passion of the Christ*, you get the idea of what went down during the crucifixion of our Savior. If you've haven't yet seen the movie, it is a must watch. Go see it. Every time He was hit, kicked, punched, spit on, pressed with thorns, had His clothing ripped and was called names, is an example of how Jesus embraced all of our failures on the cross. Jesus was the clutch it took for us to have a chance at eternal life. He gave us purpose. God could have just given up on us, but He didn't. Therefore, why would you ever give up on yourself? When I talk about embracing failure, I am urging you not to stay stuck. I am saying don't just think about the small things. Look at the bigger picture too. God put you here for a reason and purpose, so no failure you experienced or caused could ever be big enough for you to stop going.

POOR JUDGEMENT LEADS TO FAILURE

I spoke earlier about how Bill Gates, Walt Disney, Oprah Winfrey, and even Jesus embraced failure. I will now talk about how I handled the times in my life, when I felt that I had failed. I could easily tell you about a class that I failed, a test I failed, or something like that, but I want to tell you about what I like to call a "poor judgement fail."

I went to a party with one of my friends. It was Halloween night in 2013. My friend texted me and asked me if I wanted to go to a party with her that night. I immediately answered yes. She had also invited another friend of hers. We all ended up riding to the party together in her car. It was my friend, her friend and me. Keep in mind, that was a time in my life when I partied and drank heavily. When we got to the party, it ended up not really being a party. When you think of a party, you think about many people, games, drinks, and music. When we arrived, I noticed that it was just the three of us and then three guys. At first, I didn't really think too much of it. I just figured we'd stay for a little, chat, have a little fun and then leave. I am always down for a good time. When I say this happened during my heavy drinking days, I never drank in an environment like that. I would usually drink in front of people that I was comfortable with, like family or close friends. However, I never drank as irresponsibly as I did that night. One thing you must know about me, is that I was a daredevil. I was literally the one you could pretty much dare to do anything and I would be down to do it. I still like to have fun and I like to go beyond my limits. I like to be the odd girl out, so to speak. However, that night, the daredevil mentality did not work in my favor. We started to play a drinking game. One of the guys started saying things like, "I bet you can't drink that," and "You won't drink more." He was saying things like that to provoke me to show him I could. I pushed my limits, so that I would not look like a sucker. I wanted to look cool. I wanted to fit in with everyone else, so I met every one of his challenges. As a result, I drank too much. A little later that night, we all ended splitting up. We were still in the same area, but there was a girl and guy in each room. I was in a corner with a guy and we were talking, laughing and drinking. Eventually, I felt things getting foggy. I ended up making out with this guy. It was a weird feeling, because I lost control and barely knew what was going on (I'm pretty sure we've all had a drunk moment like this before). However, I can explain vividly the one thing that I do remember happening. We ended up having sex. When I woke up the next morning laying next to this guy who was a complete stranger, my automatic thoughts and feelings were of pure disgust. I felt like I had failed as a woman and I had no idea how I was going to get past this. Some people may have been okay with this scenario, but I definitely was not. I was twenty years old and had only had sex with one person by that time in my life. In addition to no longer having my virginity, my second partner was a complete stranger. This was a completely different story. I didn't even remember the guy's name the next morning. I remember crying uncontrollably that day. What made it even worse was that I was at work. I didn't want anyone to see me crying, so I kept going in and out of the bathroom and leaving to sit in my car. I kept having all these thoughts about whether I was pregnant, if the boy recorded it and showed it to someone, or just what would happen next.

I didn't know how my reputation was going to survive after this. Would I be called a slut? This may be overly dramatic, but you just have no idea what guys these days will do. They can be very cruel and careless about these things. After I cried and got past all of the random thoughts that raced through my mind, I knew that I had to get over it. It happened. It was over and I just couldn't dwell on it forever.

Have you ever had something happen to you that you so badly wish did not happen, you just placed it in the back of your mind and pretend that it didn't happen? Well, that's what I did. I forgot about it. I just didn't want to think about it any-more. I didn't want to embrace the fact that it happened and that I had to face the consequences of my decisions. It wasn't until months later that I decided to go to my doctor. I know that it was disgusting I waited that long. However, I really tried to convince myself that that whole night never even happened. What came next, killed me. I went to the doctor and got test-ed. Most women know that when you visit the gynecologist, if they don't call you back it means everything is good. When they do call you back, it means that something is wrong. About three or four days after my visit, I got a call from my doctor. She said that she was sending over a script to my pharmacy for me, because I had chlamydia. I said, "Excuse me?" I thought that I didn't hear her correctly, but then, she said it again. I got the call while I was at work, so I had to hold back my tears. However, I was devastated. I already had to deal with the fact that I had slept with a complete stranger, and now I had to deal with having an STD. I just never thought I would have to deal with something like that. I was beyond disgusted.

I went and got the medicine as soon as I could, followed up with my doctor again, and hoped and prayed that she didn't call me back. Once I noticed she didn't call back within two full weeks, I knew I was cleared. It was a sense of relief. As crazy as it sounds, although chlamydia was what came out of this situation, I had to embrace it. I had to embrace the fact that it could have been worse. I could have gotten pregnant by someone I did not know, or I could have contracted HIV, or something else that cannot be cured. I kept thinking of the what ifs. I ultimately embraced the fact that it was what it was, no matter how bad. I knew that I needed to go through reflecting on that night and its consequences, in order to ensure that I did not make the same mistake again.

Embracing your failures is not just about accepting them, it is also about making sure that you learn from the failure in such a way that you choose to try your hardest to never put yourself in the predicament again.

Embrace Failure

LET'S REFLECT
DAY #2

People measure success in many different ways. A person can even "look" like success. With the current social media, one picture or video can determine whether someone is successful. We all, at some point, look at successful people and think to ourselves, " I want to be like them". We find ourselves craving the success that they have and the life they live, forgetting the roadblocks and failures they've had to endure to lead to their success. Whether we want to believe it or not, every successful person has failed more than once. Many have even failed over 100 times. The power behind a successful person is not "Not Failing." It is the power they have to know and learn how to embrace their failure. It can be easy to forget how much they've suffered and what they've gone through to get to where they are now. We all experience failure. It is very important how we respond to the failure, that will determine our next steps and how far we will go.

PROVERBS 16:3

REFLECTION QUESTIONS

1. Has there ever been a time where you looked at a person who was successful and who seemed to have had it all together? You then met them and heard their story and were completely astonished. Explain what lesson you have learned about this.

____

____

____

____

2. What failures do you believe are holding you back and keeping you from moving forward? What are some different ways you can respond to your failure, in order to persevere?

____

____

____

____

Chapter 3

LET GO

UNDERSTAND LETTING GO

If you're around my age (25+), you should know that there are some things in life that are specific and particular to one's life experiences, while other things are universal. Some things are inevitable and some things are evitable. Is "Letting Go" considered inevitable or the evitable? Whether you're a human or an animal, letting go is hard. Whether you're 40 years old or five years old, letting go is still hard. Whether you consider yourself to be a hardcore, careless person or a gentle, caring person, guess what? Letting go is still hard. No matter what the circumstances, letting go of something we see as very important is always hard. Unfortunately, the devastating feeling of letting go of something that is important to us does not discriminate. It could even be letting go of something small. Even though letting go is something that we all usually try to avoid, the most important lesson that you will probably learn in life is the importance of the process of letting go.

We all have to deal with letting go, whether we have to let go of people close to us, plans we've made, people-pleasing behaviors, self-critical thinking or my personal favorite, spending too much money. Sometimes it feels like we have to let go of everything all at the same time. Don't think that the difficulty in letting go is always due to the fact that the actual thing that we need to release is significant. We can find it difficult to let go of a potato chip that fell on the floor after opening the bag, or to give away a pair of jeans we've had for many years but cannot fit into anymore, is hard to do. This sounds silly, but it happens. No matter what, letting go is a process. One of my favorite pastors, Michael Todd, always refers to the word process as a curse word. He talks about how nobody ever wants to go through "the process," and explains that we really must learn to trust "the process."

When finding the courage to let go of some things in our lives, we must trust the process and be patient because being processed takes time. When you are being processed, you're rejecting a negative habit and taking it out of your daily routine. You're letting go of the picture in your mind of what you believed something was or of what you wanted it to be.

My pastor, Dr. Dharius Daniels, preached a series called *Moving On*. He spoke on a specific subject entitled, "Moving on from the life you thought you wanted." One of the key points that he mentioned, while preaching this, that really made me think was one of the critical keys to an unpredictable life, is learning how to manage what you don't see coming. We can't prepare to let go of the things we don't see coming, because well, we don't see them coming.

LET GO OF PLANNING YOUR ENTIRE LIFE OUT

I've dealt with letting go of many things in my life, but there's a specific aspect of letting go I've dealt with that is worth sharing. It is the overwhelming idea that I could **plan my whole life out**! The freedom and joy that I experienced when I finally decided to let that idea go, is actually what motivated me to write this book. As I mentioned, most of us start planning at an early age. I planned what age I wanted to get married, how many kids I would have, where I would live, what kind of house I would buy and many other things. Anything that had to do with the future, I planned for it. I am positive that some of you have done the same thing. As I got older, I started to plan years in advance. To be more specific, I started saying things like, "In five years, I'll have this and that," or "In two years I'll be finished school." It doesn't matter what you have planned for the next two hours or the next two years. You must always be ready for change. You must always be ready for things to turn out the complete opposite of what you had planned.

As you know by now, I am a planner. I am not telling you that it is bad to plan. That is definitely not true. However, I am telling you it is bad to be too attached to that plan, so you close your mind to other options and opportunities. If you do this, you will drown in devastation, when your plans hit a dead end. Do you want to know why most of our plans hit a dead end, don't work out, or just fail completely? Sometimes, our plans fail, because we don't fully consult God about His larger plan for our lives. We try to plan all by ourselves and neglect the reality that we need to include God in all areas of our lives. Frankly, sometimes we flat out forget that His plan is much better than ours.

We have to stop being so wrapped up in planning our lives out. We have to let God have control.

You don't have to actually allow God to control your life—unless you want to. Only when you trust that His plan is better than your own, can you let go. The Bible says in Jeremiah 29:11, "I know the plans I have for you, declares the Lord, plans to prosper you and not to harm you, plans to give you hope and a future." In this verse, God specifically tells you that *He has plans for you*. Since He has plans for you, why are you intercepting them?

Trust me, I am asking you and I am also speaking directly to myself. I am on the other side of this book, just like you. I am always trying to interrupt what He has planned for me. Let me tell you, besides the fact that it took me some time to buckle down and actually work up to my potential in school, the results of my hard work still have not completely transpired.

My first graduation date was supposed to be in May 2018 -- was "supposed" to be. Then, May 10, 2019 was "supposed" to be my exact graduation date and year. Let's just talk about the fact that as I'm writing this, I still do not have a bachelor's degree in my hand. I remember my first semester at my university. I was very excited to attend. My first semester went very well. About a month before the semester ended, I got hit with an email saying that I owed $10,000. Unfortunately, I didn't have the money. Therefore, I had to find another option. To make things even more challenging, my credit was terrible and a loan was not an option. After trying to fix the problem for weeks, I was finally able to get a Parent Plus Loan with the help of my father. Thanks Dad! Not only did that loan cover the rest of the semester, but it covered the whole year. Won't He do it?

Yes, He will! Therefore, my first year was covered and I finished that year. It was in God's plan. I then hit another glitch during my second year that resulted in the same exact problem. When I ran into the first glitch, I really didn't have a plan. However, this time, I had a plan in place. I just knew I had it all figured out. I prayed and prayed but to my surprise, when I executed my plan, it failed! I was very confused. I could not understand why this was happening to me again. I was extremely stressed out and frustrated. I got on my knees and just asked God to make it work. I had worked so hard to get to that point in my education, that the problem I faced had sent my frustration levels off the charts. When I get frustrated, I also get much more determined and more aggressive about making a plan that works. At that point, all of my plans to finish school failed. However, I would not sit around and cry about it. I decided instead to let go of the idea that I had to finish school by a specific date. I couldn't let my self-imposed deadline to graduate keep stressing me out or holding me back. I had to trust God and find the positive in my situation, no matter how much I wanted my original plan to work. I started looking at my situation in a different way. I didn't finish school as planned, but I'd matured in many ways. I didn't finish school yet. However, I'd been able to prepare in other areas of my life, so that when I do return to school, I will be more spiritually, mentally and emotionally prepared. I didn't finish school yet. That actually gave me time to write this book. Because I haven't yet finished school, I am now able to encourage other people who run into the same problem that I did. As a result, I became less dependent on a diploma and much more dependent on God. I decided to take my situation, turn it around and use it for my good.

This should encourage you to always think positively and to look for the good in difficult situations. We do want to set deadlines and timelines, but God doesn't follow our timelines. He follows His. The Bible says in Jeremiah 1:5, "Before I formed you in the womb, I knew you; Before you were born, I sanctified you; I ordained you a prophet to the nations." If you keep this scripture in mind, you will always remember that God already knew what you would go through before he even created you. He knew I would not graduate this year, even though I just knew I would. Know that what you experience and go through, can always help someone else and trust me, they need it.

Let Go

LET'S REFLECT
DAY #3

We all have to deal with letting go of things, whether it's letting go of people close to us, plans we've made, people pleasing, self-critical thinking, or my favorite one, which is overspending. Sometimes it can even be letting go of everything at the same time. Don't think too deeply about this, you can also deal with having to let go of a chip that falls on the floor after you first open the bag, or even a pair of jeans you've had for years and years that you cannot fit into anymore. This sounds silly, yes . . . but it happens. No matter what, letting go is a process.

Forget the former things; do not dwell on the past.
See, I am doing a new thing! Now it springs up;
do you not perceive it? I am making a way in the
wilderness and streams in the wasteland.

ISAIAH 43: 18-19

REFLECTION QUESTIONS

1. Think of a time you had to let go of something drastic, that
    ended up causing you to have a major shift. (It could be a
    job, a place you lived, etc.)

____

____

____

____

2. Take yourself back to a time you had to let go of a romantic
    relationship or encounter, where holding on was hurting
    you way more than letting go. What has this experience
    taught you? Do you believe the outcome of you letting go
    was the best one, now that you look back on it?

____

____

____

____

Chapter 4

EMBRACE REALITY

FACE REALITY

How can we deal with losing ourselves, embracing failure and letting go and still be able to become our best selves? Is it even possible?

Surprisingly, some of the lowest moments in our lives can turn into the best moments of our lives. Some of the saddest feelings we've ever felt, can lead to the happiest joys we will ever feel. When struggling with the worst parts of ourselves, we can find our best selves. However, in order to step into our best selves, we must learn how to embrace everything. We must learn to embrace it all. I'm positive that this was the case for me. When most people think of the word embrace, they think of holding something or someone close. Embracing is normally used in the context of reaching out to grab or hold onto good things. We don't really refer much to embracing our weak or sad moments. I mean who wants to remember and hold their weaknesses close? Well, embracing the not so good moments, can lead to some of the greatest moments in your life. I'm sure you've heard the popular saying, "With every good, comes some bad." Well, don't forget that the opposite is also true. With every bad, comes some good.

What can haunt you more than a bad dream? YOUR PAST. How you decide to process your past regrets or difficulties can destroy you, if you let it. Michael Todd said in one of his sermons,

> *You're supposed to confront the past, learn from the past, and deal with the past, but never live there. The past, no matter how good it was or how bad it was, is the prison of your present and the purgatory of your potential.*

The dark places of your past are only a threat, when you get stuck living there. When you start basing your present decisions on past mistakes, you will always be several steps behind. You cannot move forward with a backwards mindset. This may sound cliché, but your state of mind is very powerful. Once you start thinking about something a lot, it becomes true to you in your mind. Eventually, you will start to live out what you think about. If you think you're not good enough, you will start accepting less than you deserve. If you think you'll never lose weight, you will lose hope, fail to change your diet and workout. If you start thinking your life will never change, you will remain stagnant. Most importantly, if you don't start thinking and believing in yourself the way God sees and believes in you, you will struggle with stepping into your best self.

There are many things I've done in the past that, if I did not have the proper mindset about, could hold me hostage and rob me of my future. However, I will not let that happen. I used to look back and wish I could make many changes. I would revisit certain moments, wishing that I could change the outcome. Many people go around saying "No regrets, just lessons learned." However, let's be honest. It actually takes a while to get into that state of mind. I used to tell myself no regrets all the time, but I honestly have not always meant it. Deep inside, I wanted to go back I wanted to change many things. Now, when I say no regrets, I truly mean it. My past has literally shaped who I am. There is nothing that I would go back and change.

Like many others, my past was not always the best. I can remember things from my past like they happened yesterday. However, I can also push them into the far spaces of my mind and pretend that they never happened. As hard as it is, we have to learn to face reality in order to move forward.

Starting at around the age of eight, I had been unwillingly touched sexually by three people. They were all people that I knew and was close to. I've never spoken about this with anyone before. However, I just want you to know that if this is something you've gone through, or are currently going through, you are not alone. It does not define who you are. Equally important, if this is something that you've gone through and you've been trying to simply forget about it, like I did, you don't have to be afraid to face it. I know that there are many women and men who have had this happen to them. It is only rarely discussed. Unfortunately, when abuse of this nature is spoken about, it is often in a condescending or accusatory way that makes the victim of the unwanted touch, feel as if he or she has to defend themselves. Being violated can take away your control and leave you wanting to regain your power. I remember wanting these people to stop but feeling like I could not say it. I was afraid. I felt that because they had more power and control than I had, what I said wouldn't matter.

Whether something happened to you years ago or yesterday, face your thoughts and feelings, so that you don't end up imprisoned by them. Find a friend you can talk to about what happened to you. Let your emotions out. Tell someone how you feel. Get a journal and write it out. You can even tear out the pages and destroy what you wrote if you want to. Whatever you have to do to get the trauma out of your mind and face your feelings, do it. Sometimes you just have to face the facts. Even though you may not want to believe it, BELIEVE IT. It happened. It's over. You overcame it. Now you can move on.

COMMON SETBACKS

There are some things that are considered to be common setbacks which can cause us to get off track on our paths to becoming our best selves.

INSECURITY

I would argue that being insecure is one of the biggest obstacles that keeps you from stepping into your best self. Insecurity can get in the way of everything. Many times our insecurities cannot be controlled. Being insecure can be manifested in small, medium and big ways. Some insecurities take much longer to go away or to be overcome than others. The best way to get past insecurities, is to embrace them. Whether it's the owner of Chick-fil-a, the pastor of a church, or the richest person on earth, everyone deals with insecurities.

Look at your insecurities as differences. Most of the time, we look at our insecurities as weaknesses, because we don't think that others have the same traits we fault ourselves for having. Look at these shortcomings as hallmarks of your unique path, instead of as parts of yourself that make you terrible. If you do this, you will start to see your insecurities much differently.

I personally struggle daily with the insecurity of being rejected. I worry, at times, about not being accepted. It doesn't matter whether it is by a person, job, God, stranger, etc. I can be very insecure about being accepted. This may sound like a common insecurity, but it is much deeper for me. In my experience, the insecurity of rejection makes me constantly question myself, my worth, my abilities and everything. I sometimes start to have thoughts along the lines of "If this person doesn't like this or that about me, then it must not be good." Sometimes the insecurity makes me think, "If I can't get this job, then maybe I'm just not good enough for it. " As a result, I start to think too much about what I can change or do differently. Don't get me started on people. We often think that when a person rejects us, betrays us, or just simply walks away from us, that there is something wrong with us. Thinking that way minimizes our self-worth and keeps us from moving forward. The way I try to deal with this insecurity, is by constantly affirming myself. I constantly focus on things that I know I'm good at. They are the things that make me who I am. -I practice seeing myself the way God sees me. When I reset my thinking in this way, I realize that I'm just here to help everyone else. However, I have to help myself. I have also come to the conclusion that I am a perfectionist. I always strive for the best. I hate to accept less, so I constantly have to remind myself that I am just not perfect, and that I never will be.

FRIENDSHIPS AND RELATIONSHIPS

Many of us often let friendships and relationships get in the way of us moving forward. We believe that the way others love us is an indication of our worth. We put others on a very high pedestal and expect them to

L O V E us so much, that we forget that we need to learn how to L O V E ourselves first. At the end of the day, it all starts with us.

We tend to think that the way we act will determine someone else's

L O V E for us. However, in reality, if someone loves you unconditionally, they will look past your flaws, weaknesses and insecurities. Their goal is to help you grow and become the best version of yourself. Their love should cause you to see beautiful things about yourself, that you didn't even know were inside of you.

> *BUT WAIT, DO NOT TAKE SOMEONE*
> *WHO LOVES YOU FOR GRANTED. THIS IS*
> *BECAUSE SOMEONE WHO LOVES YOU IS*
> *ABSOLUTELY ALLOWED TO WALK AWAY*
> *FROM YOU.*

Just because someone loves you, does not mean they have to tolerate you. Loving from a distance is a real thing. I struggle in this area of my life, because despite that I love harder than you'd ever imagine, I can also be very closed, when it comes to showing my emotions, flaws and insecurities. Yes, I love hard! As a result, I rarely ever let people go. Someone can hurt me to the core and I will still find a way to keep loving them, forgiving them and helping them. I don't let people go easily, because I never believed in walking away from people. However, believe me when I say that I'm learning. I am the one who believes in giving people many chances. I am the one who is always saying that people can change and that there's always good inside of someone. This has been my biggest downfall. You probably think my ability to forgive is a good thing. For the most part, it is. However, like I said before, learning how to love from a distance is a real thing and sometimes you just need to love people from afar.

Everyone cannot go where you are going. Everyone is not healthy for you. Learn to put people in their place. Like my pastor, Dharius Daniels once said, *"It's not that you have the wrong people in your life, it's that you have them in the wrong place."*

I have been praying to God for much better discernment in my life, when it comes to my relationships. I pray that He teaches me to love people from a distance. I pray that He gives me the strength to love better, to love selflessly, unconditionally and in ways that are much more healthy.

Mistakes

It doesn't matter how perfect you think you are. You have made mistakes. Not just one or two, but millions (maybe even more). Mistakes shape us into who we are. We have to make mistakes, in order to grow. Never stop loving yourself and believing that you cannot move forward, because of a mistake that you have made. Never let the gravity of a mistake define you. Instead, after you make a mistake, practice this cycle:

1. Think about it
2. Pray about it.
3. Learn from it.
4. Move on.

COMPARISONS

Comparing myself to others has been very harmful to me. The cure of comparing visits me from time to time. No matter what I do , I still end up comparing myself to others. At one point, even scrolling on social media became a headache. Looking at what everyone was doing and saying, made me feel as if nothing I did was ever enough. I never seemed to feel 100% secure. I always felt like I needed to be giving more or that I just needed to be more.

I was insecure. I had made mistakes. I had failed friendships and relationships. I struggled to stop comparing myself to others. These things impacted my level of self-confidence. Everyone around me was always saying "Jalia, you're so confident." I would always just smile and think, "If only you knew."

All of these things can be blockers that set you back and stop you from becoming your best self. However, there are many people around you, who also struggle with these issues and situations. At one time in my life, these things started to completely take over me. I always knew I was different and unique. It definitely took me some time. However, I've learned to just relax and enjoy my own race, because I've grown to realize that uniqueness is a very beautiful thing. Once I started to embrace every single flaw that made me insecure, they eventually became beautiful in my eyes. I started to embrace where I am.

We must learn to embrace our mistakes. It is admittedly very hard to embrace a mistake you made, when you knew that what you were doing was not right. I call these the "you know what you're doing mistakes." These kinds of situations bother me most. This is because I always think, "I could have definitely avoided that." Thankfully, the one person who will always forgive us is God. The Bible gives me the most hope, when it comes to embracing my past, my insecurities, my friendships and relationships and my mistakes because, believe me if you've ever read the Bible, those people were a hot mess and God still used them for good. Knowing this reminds me that no matter how much of a mess I am, God will still use me.

Learn to embrace everything in life, including the good, the bad and the ugly. Embrace every obstacle, mistake, insecurity, relationship, setback, struggle and past experience. In the end, let your life be a story that ends well. Remember that anytime God gets involved in something, He improves it. If it's not better, He's not done. Believe me, God is not done with you yet.

Embrace Reality

LET'S REFLECT
DAY #4

Surprisingly, some of the lowest moments in our lives can turn into the best moments of our lives. Some of the saddest feelings we've ever felt, can lead to the happiest joy we will ever feel. While struggling with the worst parts of ourselves, we can find our best selves. However, in order to step into our best selves, we must learn how to embrace. This involves embracing everything. We must learn to embrace it all. I'm positive that this was the case for me. When most people think of the word "Embrace", they think of holding something close, supporting something or someone close to them, or just simply enjoying a specific moment. Embracing is normally only tied to the good things. We don't really refer to embracing our weak or bad moments most of the time. I mean who wants to really remember their weak moments? Well, Embracing the not so good moments can lead to some of the greatest moments in your life. I'm sure you've heard the popular saying, "With every good comes some bad". Well don't forget the opposite of that saying. Therefore, with every bad comes good.

ROMANS 8:28

REFLECTION QUESTIONS

1. "Embracing the not so good moments can lead to some of
   the greatest moments in your life." Reflect on some not so
   good moments that you actually embraced that ended up
   leading to some of your greatest moments. What made you
   embrace it at the time, even though it looked ugly?

   ____

   ____

   ____

   ____

2. Write one sentence about the future of your life changing
   the narrative from good to great.

   ____

   ____

   ____

   ____

Chapter 5

ALONE

FEAR OF LONELINESS

Close your eyes and imagine something for a moment. I know that everyone can't remember everything. However, I am sure that there is a memory that we can all vividly recall. I know that I can. This is a day that I counted down the days for. I dreamed of this day. When it finally came, I was the happiest little kid on earth. I was like a kid in Disney World. That was very corny but imagine kindergarten. It is your first day of school. You walk into kindergarten with your flashy bookbag and matching lunch box. Your hair is in your favorite style and your outfit is matching from head to toe. You tried to rush breakfast in the morning, so you still have a smudge of grape (well, in my case, strawberry) jelly on the side of your mouth from the toast you ate. However, you are not even thinking about it, because the only thing you're thinking about, is whether everyone will like you. You are hoping that people will want to be your friend and that your teacher will think you're the smartest kid ever. You want the coolest kid to share a cubby next to yours. You also want to be named student of the month, so your picture can be posted in the classroom. You want all of the other kids to notice you. Let's not get started on lunch time. You want to be surrounded by several kids at the "cool table." You want to be "The Cool Kid", "The Popular Kid", and "The Well-Known Kid." There's no doubt we all want attention at that age. It's almost like we feel more complete, if others like us and we are popular. This feeling of wanting to be liked and not wanting to be alone, stems from childhood for most of us. It also starts earlier for some of us. Many of us initially genuinely have an unwillingness to be alone. We just don't want to be by ourselves, feel left out or unwanted. Sometimes the feeling goes away and sometimes it doesn't. Interestingly, it doesn't matter how young or old a person is. Most people have gone through a phase of loneliness that caused them, at some point, to try to fill a void with unwanted and unneeded people or things.

I often go through phases of feeling alone. Like many people, my feelings of aloneness turn on and off. There have been times when I've had many people around me and I still felt alone. There were times when I actually had people say, "I am here for you," knew they meant it and I still felt alone. Feelings of being alone just come randomly. No matter how many people you have around you, it can still be inevitable and scary.

DEPRESSED AGAIN

My most recent bout with feeling alone was not pretty. It was the summer of 2018. I again found myself in a very deep depression. I did not want to get out of bed at all. I felt very helpless and my emotions were taking over my life. In my job, I was working doubles after doubles, while smiling and laughing like nothing was wrong with me. I was actually falling completely apart inside. There wasn't really anyone I could talk to, because most of what I was feeling I couldn't even explain—or I just didn't want to.

Things got so bad during that summer, I seriously contemplated suicide. I planned it out in my head and sadly, I came very close to carrying out that plan. I felt very weak and unimportant. I constantly asked myself, "Why be here?" I cried so much, that I started to get constant headaches. All of the stress caused me to miss my menstrual cycle for a month. I finally went to my doctor, because I started to get worried. It was very bad.

I can now look back at that time in my life with the confidence and power. I can declare, "Yes that was a scary and difficult season that I went through. However, I overcame it and did not let it defeat me." It was during this time that I truly sought God. I began to invest more time getting to know Him more. I learned God's true purpose for allowing us to go through seasons of darkness. He will often take everything and everyone away to get us to fully focus on Him. If you ever see or hear me speak about God "too much," "too often" or "too aggressively," it is because surviving this season in my life increased my love and appreciation for God very much. To those who do not know my story, how I speak about God just may seem like "too much." Thank you, depression! I could have been dead sleeping in my grave . . . but God.

CHOOSE CAREFULLY

There is no doubt that God wants us to have relationships with people. We need to form relationships. However, please *do not* choose relationships out of loneliness. Choosing to connect with the wrong types of people is easy to do, when you're in this state of mind. Do not look for people to fill your empty, lonely void.

Even when we are not lonely, we must carefully choose our relationships. Jesus had many relationships, but He only walked very closely with a few people. He had twelve disciples, but He only walked closely with three: Peter, James and John. He was very specific about who he chose. The relationships that you form, whether intimate, business, or friendly, must be formed with care. Be very aware and selective about the people you choose. The people you choose to walk with, should add value to your life. Do not choose people who make you feel like you are still alone. Believe me, they are out there.

You should frequently sit back and take an inventory of who is in your life. Ask yourself questions like, "What am I getting out of this relationship?" "Is this relationship helping me grow? "Is it pushing me to become the best version of myself?" You should also flip the script and ask yourself those same exact questions about the type of friend you are to others. While we all must realize that relationships will never be perfect, we must make sure that you are not confusing dead-end relationships that should be let go of, with relationships that are good for us. However, they may make you feel uncomfortable, because the person is helping you to grow, step into your full potential and become your best self.

You are allowed to give people grace. You are allowed to forgive people and give them chances. However, what you are not allowed to do, is pause your journey in the process. There are people who you can love from a distance. Sometimes, that is just what you have to do. Family can be among the people you must also love from a distance. Don't ever feel bad for detaching from people who are not adding to your purpose, draining you, or who constantly remind you of who you used to be. This is especially important when they are not helping you get to who you will be. We have all had some relationships that we have needed to let go of. It is always hard to let go of something that you thought was real. When you expect something from someone, you're not as surprised and it doesn't hurt as much. However, have you ever had to let go of someone you trusted very much? Have you ever had to let go of someone you would never have expected to treat you the way they did? That is very hurtful. It literally feels like a stab in the back (not just metaphorically) but physically too. Just remember, everyone is not meant to be in your life forever. There are seasons in our lives, in which certain people belong and certain people don't. Not everyone is called to go where you are going. That is completely okay. I've lost many things and people in the last year. This year that I almost named my year, "Jalia's Losses," but instead I named it "Jalia's gain."

EMBRACE BEING ALONE

When you learn to embrace being alone, you stop accepting less than you deserve. You start accepting what you know you deserve. Even though relationships are important, it is more important to understand and appreciate the purpose of aloneness. I don't believe in being someone else's other half or in anyone completing me. That's why I don't speak in terms of making someone my everything or anything like that. I believe in doing the work to be whole by myself. It is my job to work to be my strongest self every day. No human will ever be my everything, because God is my everything and my God is a jealous God. The most I can do, is let a person compliment me and add to my greatness. However, that is all.

Do not get so caught up in your relationships, that you start to rely on another person for your happiness, goals, character, dignity, relationship with God and your self-esteem. This is because you start to put too much responsibility on the other person to make you whole. When you realize that the person is not capable of giving you everything you desire, you are inevitably ready to quickly walk away from the relationship. This is true, even if it's not time. In reality, most of what you desire, must first come from within. For example, someone can tell you you're nice looking all day. However, if you don't feel beautiful when you look in the mirror, it won't mean as much. A person can go to extreme measures to make you happy. However, if you don't dig deep to find happiness within yourself, you won't be happy. Tying your happiness to another person, means that if they ever leave you, they will take your happiness with them.

Listen to me! There is nothing wrong with enjoying and embracing your alone time. It is not weird to do things by yourself. Take trips by yourself, go out to eat by yourself, invest in yourself, start that business by yourself, read books and do research, so that you can learn how to strategize. There are many things that you can do during your alone time, so never discredit it. During your alone time, you should be consistently preparing yourself to be the best relationship partner for all of your current relationships and for the new relationships that you will form. Use your time alone wisely. Refill, refresh, and rejuvenate yourself. Remember that you cannot pour from an empty cup.

Alone

LET'S REFLECT
DAY #5

This feeling of wanting to be liked and not wanting to be alone, began in kindergarten for most of us. For some of us, it started earlier. We genuinely had an unwillingness to be alone. We just don't want it. Sometimes the feeling goes away, while other times it doesn't. Unfortunately, it doesn't matter how young or old a person is, most of us have already gone through a phase of loneliness that has caused us at some point to try and fill an empty void with unwanted and unneeded things or people.

Be strong and courageous. Do not be afraid or
terrified because of them, for the LORD your God
goes with you; he will never leave you
nor forsake you.

DEUTERONOMY 31:6

REFLECTION QUESTIONS

1. When was the last time you were really alone? How did it make you feel? Can you honestly say you embrace your aloneness or are you constantly searching for company?

____

____

____

____

2. Be honest. Is God enough in your life right now? If your answer is anything other than yes, plan out some time that you can spend with just you and God. It doesn't have to be long periods of time. You can start with a short amount of time.

____

____

____

____

Chapter 6

IMPERFECTIONS

LIFE AS A PERFECTIONIST

Some things are good. Some things are bad. And some things are bittersweet. Yes! Bitter, yet sweet. Well, trying to be perfect is bittersweet.

In my experience, being a perfectionist can be described as being upset that you earned a 99% on a test, because you know you could have gotten a 100%. Perfectionist tendencies make you want to "dot your i's and cross your t's all the time. You beat yourself up over the smallest mistakes and setbacks. You take longer than necessary to complete tasks, because you're so focused on perfecting it during the process, rather than just completing it and then going back and editing it later. You place unrealistic standards on yourself. You can get really discouraged by unmet goals. You have an "all or nothing" approach to everything. You think more deeply about situations that others would simply examine and take at face value. You're disappointed by anything less than perfection. You get so caught up in worrying about doing something imperfectly, that it leads to procrastination. Then you end up doing nothing at all. You have a very specific way of how you want things done. You always focus very closely on the end result.

I know the perfectionist in me didn't cover everything. However, I'm sure that you get the point by now. Being a perfectionist is not all bad. It can actually be a very positive thing, but there are times when it becomes a major problem.

It becomes a problem when you start to develop a huge fear of failure that leads to frequent self-doubt.

You should want the best for yourself. You should strive for perfection. You should have high standards. However, you should not get so caught up, that you forget that no matter how many times you get in the car on the road to perfection, you will never get there.

You won't get there because nobody is perfect. Nothing will ever be perfect. Everyone's picture of what perfect is, is different.

Instead, do your best. That's all that matters.

Don't get me wrong, it's okay to take a break sometimes. It's okay to take a step back from the maddening "I need to make this perfect" world. Maybe you can just be "normal" sometimes. Believe me, I know it's hard, but things just don't always go as planned. Improvisation is necessary.

The last couple years of my life have been a prime example of improvisation. I've had to learn to go with the flow more than ever before.

I am a planner. I set a goal. I figure out how I'm going to achieve that goal.

Then I plan. I plan. And I plan some more.

I have learned, however, that God will come in and interrupt our plans, so that He can execute His plan. God already had plans for us, before we were even a thought in our parent's mind. We can't question what He had already planned to do. The bottom line is, stop trying to be so perfect all the time. Trust and follow God and He will lead you into all the right things.

Being a perfectionist is the hardest thing in the world. However, what's even harder is coming to the realization that nothing and no one is P E R F E C T. Remember that you are as perfect as you're going to get and you are perfect being imperfect!

GET PICTURE PERFECT OUT OF MY HEAD

Naively speaking, when I first gave my life to God over a decade ago, I thought that it was a ticket to an easier, simpler and less complicated life. Little did I know, I was in for a major surprise. I knew the power of salvation, but not the ugly catastrophes that it came with. Being an imperfect Christian and a millennial who loves God, is like being a celebrity. It's like being in the spotlight and being carefully judged every single time you make a mistake or aren't living in a perfect little bubble. The world will repeatedly say that they want your transparency, honesty, the most authentic and uncensored you. However, you learn that unless you're living "perfectly," they really don't and won't accept the true you. There are many times throughout my life when I heard, "Jalia can't do that because she goes to church," or "Don't say or do that around Jalia, because she goes to church." On many occasions, I wanted to just stop being who I was for a moment. I wanted to live what seemed to be a more normal life. I wanted to be accepted as normal and just wanted to be able to fit in with everyone else. I wanted, for once, to not have to be known as the "Christian girl." I know this was dishonoring, but it's the absolute truth. There was a long period during which I wanted to change who I was. However, as the endless love and grace of God confirmed many times, He didn't create me to be like everyone else. He didn't create me to be normal. He created me to live for him, while being imperfect. He created me to be an example. He created me to stand out. I've come to absolutely love being imperfect. Giving your life to Christ doesn't mean that everything will automatically be good. It simply means that you will never have to walk alone. God won't keep the storms from coming. However, when the storms come, with the word, love, and grace of God, you'll still be able to stand and not fall.

Thank you, Jesus for keeping me, even when I didn't want to be kept. I now desire to reach my full potential and the amazing purpose that you have for my life through pure authenticity.

AN IMPERFECT CHURCH

I grew up in a Pentecostal (traditional) church for most of my life. I was two years old, when my parents joined the church. Of course, they told me that, because otherwise I wouldn't remember. What I do remember is that I gave myself to God at eleven years old. Yes, I was young. However, I had a very strong understanding and love for God. I knew that giving my life to Him is what I wanted to do. I spent a lot of time with some of my family and friends praying, reading, having church and making up dances. I was what most people would call "on fire for God." The major problem that I had in my relationship with Him during that time in my life, however, was that I did not have a correct understanding of God's grace. I believed that every time that I messed up, "I wasn't saved anymore." I would probably say that I got saved a hundred or more times.

As time went on, I started to grow apart from my home church. Although I had no idea why, I just knew it wasn't really the place for me anymore. It just no longer felt like home anymore. I loved my church. I just couldn't understand why I was getting the feeling that I needed to leave. I would go every single Sunday and be upset, if I had to miss a Sunday. I barely liked to visit other churches, because I just wanted to be at my church. I was also very involved in church activities. However, praise dancing was my thing. I praise danced all of my life. This was the way I expressed myself. This was a stress reliever. I just loved to dance. I wanted to attend every single church event and was very eager to learn.

Overall, I was very used to going to church (my church in particular) and I never knew that I would eventually start to feel out of place there. It started to feel very stagnant and routine, rather than growth oriented. At one point, I started feeling like I was going just to go. Therefore, I stopped going altogether. Over time, I started to visit other churches with friends, family members and even alone. I've visited some good churches, but nothing felt like home. I eventually stopped attending church completely and even started to work on Sundays. My father would ask me questions like, "Why haven't you been to church?" or "What made you stop going?" I could sense that he knew something was wrong, because, like I said, "I've always loved church!" There was ultimately nothing that was keeping me from attending church, besides the fact that I just felt out of place and I had not found somewhere else that I could call home. I felt uncomfortable, disconnected, lost and confused. I still had a connection with God but it started to slowly fall apart. I started to strongly rebel. I started to regularly do things I never used to do at all. I knew something needed to change.

At the beginning of 2018, I started visiting the church that I attend now. I was invited by my friend, who I grew up with at my previous church. The very first time I came, I knew it was different than most of the other churches I'd visited. When I first started to attend, I would come to the campus, which was about an hour away from me. I did not care about the distance. I just knew I had to be there. The more I attended, the more I knew that it was the place for me. I knew that I had finally found my new church home. I was so excited, because it had been almost four years since I'd felt like I belonged somewhere.

I decided to make the decision to join the church in the summer of 2018. I attended church every week for almost a year. I grew like never before. I am not saying that you can only grow and work on your relationship with God, by consistently attending church. However, believe me, it is a beautiful feeling when you can grow with a community of believers. I am currently stepping into my best self ever. My relationship with God has flourished. I have participated in several learning groups. I've taken leaps of faith that I'd always been afraid to take and I plan to become even more involved. There's much more that I could elaborate on. However, if I had to describe all I've learned while attending this church so far, it would be to "Have Faith" and to be "Transparent."

I've had to trust God with many things over the past year and a half. It is only the strength of my faith that has allowed me to do so. I've learned to be transparent, not only to help other people but also to show people what God can create from such a mess. I am a work in progress. However, I am very excited about what God has been doing, and for what He will continue to do in my life.

The experience of growing up in a traditional church and then attending and watching YouTube videos or listening to the podcasts of non-traditional churches, made me more aware of some of the differences and similarities that exist among churches. I want to address the three differences that most impacted me:

NON-JUDGMENTAL

I think that this is a key characteristic of the non-traditional church. They DO NOT JUDGE you at all. No matter what color, size, age, stage of life or state of mind you are in, they include and embrace you. The first time I attended a non-traditional church, it was definitely not what I expected. It was not what I was used to. When I first started attending, I felt like I always had to be in a dress and I always had to act a certain way. However, as time went on, I learned that was not the case at all. I learned that it is a completely different environment and culture, in relation to how people judge you. It allowed me to be more of myself. I did not have to cover up who I am for a day, just for the sake of tradition. I did not have to stress out about being judged.

Of course, there should be boundaries for a church setting. However, it should also be understood that not everyone who comes in, will be an angel sent from heaven. Not everyone who comes in, can look like an usher or minister. Over the years, I've had several conversations with people about church. Many of their reasons for not coming to church are because that they don't want to feel out of place. They tell stories about how uncomfortable they were. They explain how it felt to avoid the dirty looks that they received because they looked, dressed, or spoke differently than the church people. I'm not saying that you should go to church wearing booty shorts. However, you shouldn't judge someone, who is wearing an appropriate pair of jeans. Many people believe they have to change who they are, to fit into a church setting. If you think about it, wouldn't you rather get a non-saved drug dealer into church or some man or woman who doesn't already know God, rather than someone who is already a church goer? Isn't the job of the church to help those who don't believe in Christ at all? Why are traditional churches so caught up focusing on someone who backslid but is already saved? Saving that drug dealer's or non-believers' life should be the priority — not how someone is dressed. However, to accomplish that, churchgoers have to treat the drug dealer the same way they treat the members with the long dresses on.

Let's learn from God's example. God is attracted to the broken. He doesn't only call the qualified, he qualifies and equips those who answer the call. He wants people to know Him. Most of the people we read about in the Bible who God used to do miraculous things, were completely messed up. Did He pass judgement on them and render them useless? No! He didn't pass judgement on them and shut them out. He took them under his wing, looked at who they could become and transformed them. It is the same with building a business. Yes, it's good to hold onto your current customers, but what are you doing to attract new ones? At the end of the day, God loves all of us the same, no matter what. He does not judge us according to how much money is in our bank account, how many pairs of shoes we have, or anything trivial like that. He wants us to strengthen our relationship with him, live for him and love Him and others.

For a long time, I felt like I had to come to God a certain way in prayer or in order for Him to accept me. This was the same way I felt when I went to church. However, I had to learn that I can talk to God the same way I would talk to a friend. He wants us to be completely open and honest with Him. God can only change us, when we are honest about who we really are. We do not have to pretend with Him. Too many churches and too many believers focus on people having to have a certain look, rather than on drawing people closer to God. That should ultimately be the goal. We can and should be different than people who do not profess the faith, but we should also be relatable. When Jesus walked the Earth, He didn't travel with a bright light shining on Him all the time. He was not a dressed to impress kind of person. He came just like me or you. He did not deny the power that He had, but He also did not walk around acting like he was better than others. He healed people. He helped people. He prayed, just like we do. The scriptures teach us the proper perspective on judgement and yet we still judge with bad intentions.

Matthew 7:1-2 says, "Do not judge, or you too will be judged. For in the same way you judge others, you will be judged, and with the measure you use, it will be measured to you."

BIBLE BASED/PRACTICAL

Besides experiencing less judgement from the people I met and observed in non-traditional churches, I also found non-traditional churches to also be much more Bible-based and practical. As a believer, it is important to understand that you should be willing to include God in every area of your life. You should not only include Him in areas in which you feel the most comfortable, but also in areas where you feel the least comfortable. I've seen non-traditional churches speak more on topics that other churches are afraid to talk about. They are adamant about transforming people and about making sure that people come to church and get the help they actually need. The leaders in the non-traditional churches I have been exposed to, focus and preach a lot about Jesus's actual methods of doing things and less about traditions. They preach from the Bible and always back everything up with scripture. They do not only use scriptures to backup personal opinions. They try their best to give you step by step instructions on how to do everything that they teach.

As Mark 7:13 says, "So you are teaching that it is not important to do what God said. You think that it is more important to follow your own rules, which you teach people. And you do many things like that."

INNER GROWTH

Finally, non-traditional churches are very big on inner growth and change. Non-traditional churches rarely focus on the image of the church. They focus on effecting change outside of the building, rather than on spending hours and hours inside the church building and never putting time into using the information learned in church. They have more of a "Don't just hear the word, be the word" philosophy.

More contemporary fellowships are always finding ways to do things that will better the congregation. They focus more on what is going on inside of the people's minds, hearts and lives, rather than focusing on how they look on the outside. Leaders help the congregation experience transformation by making it a priority that people change their lives. In this way, they can not only be an asset inside the church, but outside of the church, by living up to the standards the Bible holds people of faith to.

For example, what good is it to have grown up in church, be in church every Sunday and still have sex outside of marriage? Doesn't that honestly defeat the purpose? If you've been in church all your life, why has there not been a change? We all sin and fall short of the glory of God. However, there is a difference between sinning and making a mistake and continuously doing what you know is wrong, because you know God will forgive. In order to live a different life, you really have to live a different life.

I had to deal with this issue in my life. Like all of us, I've had to change things that I knew were not pleasing to God but that were only pleasing to my flesh. Continuing to sin, is like worshipping the devil. I had to learn that if I truly wanted to experience spiritual and personal growth, I could not do the same things I used to do. I had to focus on being all in and not just halfway into my relationship with God. We are going to mess up a lot, but we should live our lives in a way in which people can look at us and see God. Jesus should live through us. Jesus gave us a choice to follow him or the world. It is a decision we must make for ourselves. Jesus is a gentleman. He does not force anything on us, but he does let us know what the right choice is.

As Proverbs 14:12 says, "There is a way that appears to be right, but in the end, it leads to death."

I am saying this because we really need to come together as a church and remember that we are the church. People are not leaving churches for their own personal gain. They are leaving for legitimate reasons and we must be open to address these issues to fulfill what God is calling us to do. We should be blessed to have church buildings but we also should be focused on transforming and stepping into all that God has called us to. Anyone can quote scriptures, but are we really living them? To live the faith, we have to seek God first and everything else second. God should be the center of it all. Remember how jealous He is? Even though the culture of some churches is starting to change, that doesn't mean those changes take away from what is most important-- God and His word. Times change. Things change. People change. However, there is one thing that stays the same and that is the word of God.

Imperfections

LET'S REFLECT
DAY #6

Being a perfectionist is the hardest thing in the world. However, what's even harder, is coming to the realization that nothing and nobody is PERFECT. However, remember that you are as perfect as you're going to get. You are perfect being imperfect.

*For we all stumble in many ways. And if anyone
does not stumble in what he says, he is a perfect man,
able also to bridle his whole body.*

JAMES 3:2

REFLECTION QUESTIONS

1. List some of your imperfections and then turn them into positives.

____

____

____

____

2. Why do you want to be perfect?

____

____

____

____

Chapter 7

RELATIONSHIP MATTERS

UNDERSTANDING AND BUILDING RELATIONSHIPS

Family, friends, significant others, co-workers, managers, classmates and teammates are all relationships that we go through in our lives. Whether you'd like to believe it or not, relationships make up a huge part of our lives and they affect us greatly. Because we already have specific criteria in our heads for what makes a good or bad relationship, entering relationships with people is usually much simpler than keeping them. For example, when it comes to friendships, we usually befriend people who are like us. In romantic relationships, we usually date people who are pleasing to our eyes. Building relationships is like taking a test. We sometimes think the test was nice and easy, and then we are stunned when we get the grade back and realize, "I failed!" There are also times when we think the test was very hard, but we end up doing well and earning an A.

Building relationships can be similar. Similar to the test scenario, there are times when you can wrongly judge people. It's slightly different when it comes to co-workers and managers, because we don't really pick those people. They just come with the job. Nevertheless, certain general rules and challenges that come with relating to others still apply. I think it's safe to say that every relationship in our lives has some sort of impact on our life. Sometimes that impact is very significant and other times it is less significant.

Every relationship impacts our life during the specific time when we have the most contact with the person we are in relationship with. Whether the relationship lasts for a long time or if it is short-lived, relationships also have an impact on our future. Some interactions are seasonal and some are long-lasting. When first developing relationships, you don't really know which kind of relationship it will be, until time reveals it. We don't plan for relationships to end. Due to a number of circumstances, they just do.

I really don't know how I got so blessed, but I have some of the greatest friends a person could ask for. This is why I can confidently tell you that who you have around you, is very important. Of course, I've taken some losses too. Those losses were necessary for me to take on my journey to becoming my best self. Take heed: who you choose to surround yourself with, is critical to your destiny.

LEARN WHO TO STAY AWAY FROM)

Who you choose to surround yourself with is very important. Here are four characteristics of the type of person you should probably stay away from:

DISHONEST PEOPLE

In literally any type of relationship, communication is absolutely necessary. I am a huge communicator. I mean huge. Talking things out was always a big deal for me. Believe me when I say, it's very hard to communicate with a dishonest person. A dishonest person usually doesn't know how to express the truth, so they instead react in anger. There's a saying that goes, "I can respect a bad decision, but I cannot respect a liar." Once a person lies to you, it'll be very hard to trust them the next time around. I'm not saying that second chances aren't an option, but there's a difference between forgiving someone over a mistake and forgiving someone who lied to you. A person who lies to you, clearly doesn't respect you and there is no relationship without trust.

PEOPLE WHO ALWAYS BRING UP YOUR PAST

We have all met people who are constantly reminding you of all the bad things you did or of the person you used to be. However, they never have anything to say about who you're becoming or what you're currently doing. These kinds of people are very hard to be around and to have relationships with, because it's very hard to change for the better, when you're constantly reminded of your past. I am not saying that it is bad to reflect and realize how far you've come. However, you can always tell when someone is reminding you of your less glorious days out of spite. You need to be around people who are necessary for your future and not your past. That person may have only been necessary for your past. It is important to understand that some relationships expire.

People who Pull you Away from your Relationship with God

Whether you're reading this as a Christ follower or not, there should always be something in your relationships that is uncompromisable. As a young Christian woman who is solely on the path to seek God, I cannot afford to have a relationship with someone who constantly drags me away from it. At some point, you have to be more intentional with your friendships. In my younger, less mature days, I had all types of friends around me (mainly because I am a very friendly person). However, I now make sure I'm not constantly around people who weaken my relationship with God.

A person is never solely responsible for your relationship with God. However, another person can definitely play a part in strengthening or weakening it. An example is a person who knows what you're trying to accomplish spiritually. However, they're always trying to get you to do something that is not helping you toward that goal. In that case, this person doesn't care very much about your growth. They only want to be around you, as long as you're doing what they're doing.

A Person who is Someone you Don't Want to be Like

This is honestly very simple. Why would you want to hang out with someone whose principles you don't agree with? Why would you want to hang out with someone whose character you dislike? There's nothing wrong with being around people you don't have everything in common with. However, being in close proximity with them on a daily basis is a different ball game.

I never actually believed the saying "you are who you hang around," or the scripture "bad company corrupts good character." However, I found myself in some situations I never thought I'd be in, because I was hanging with certain people. Michael Todd says, "Hang around people who gossip, hang around people who steal, hang around people who are luke-warm. You're weakening your ability to stand." Stop hanging around and building relationships with people who don't stand for the same things as you.

IT'S NOT YOUR FAULT

Relationships end. It's life and that's okay. What's not okay is blaming yourself for it. There are times when a relationship may end due to something you may have done or even said. However, that doesn't mean you're any less of a person. It's a learning experience.

When it comes to romantic relationships, there may be a person who does not want to be in a relationship with you. This doesn't mean that you're less of a person. You may be getting treated terribly by someone. A man or woman you've been dating and are madly in love with, may have been cheating on you your entire relationship. You might also have a best friend you have known for your whole life who betrayed you in ways that no one else could. When we run into these types of situations, we start asking ourselves questions. Am I not enough? Do I need to give more or less? Is there anything at all that I can change about "ME," that would have changed the outcome of this situation or the way I'm being treated? Questions like theses randomly flow through our heads, when we deal with such crazy, unexpected life matters. For some reason, whenever something bad happens we, at some point, place all of the blame for what went wrong onto ourselves. We say, "It's my fault." Even when things are far from being in our control, we turn and point the finger back at us. With this frame of thinking, our parents getting divorced turns out to be our fault. Getting molested becomes our fault. Someone cheating on us definitely always becomes our fault. Why is that? We blame ourselves, because we feel we're ultimately responsible for the outcome of a certain situation, even when someone treats you badly. However, that it is not your fault. Jesus was perfect and still got treated poorly, so let that be your reminder every time you think that it is *your fault*. Learn to end things peacefully and gracefully and stop blaming yourself for things that were totally out of your control.

Relationship Matters

LET'S REFLECT
DAY#7

For some reason, everything bad that happens usually at some point turns back to us. It's always "our" fault. Even the things that are far out of our control are turned back to us. Our parents getting divorced, turns out to be our fault. Getting molested becomes our fault. Someone cheating on us definitely always becomes our fault. Why is that? We blame ourselves, because we feel that we're ultimately responsible for the outcome of the situation. This is especially true when someone treats you badly. I'm here to tell you that it is not your fault. Jesus was perfect and still got treated poorly, so let that be your reminder every time you think that it is "you". Learn to end things peacefully and gracefully.

I have told you these things, so that in me you may have peace. In this world you will have trouble. But take heart! I have overcome the world.

JOHN 16:33

REFLECTION QUESTIONS

1. What have you been blaming yourself for? How can you refocus this energy?

____

____

____

____

2. God overcame the world. Write a list of confirmations you can keep in a notebook, put up on a wall, etc. in order to feel like a conqueror anytime you feel defeated.

____

____

____

____

Part II:

GET PREPARED

Chapter 8

STRIDING

We all know that we live in a "grinding" kind of world. Everything is all about the grind. We're literally expected to grind day in and day out. If the next person isn't grinding, they're considered lazy and characterized as not doing something right. Grinding has become so normal in some circles, that anything else seems out of the ordinary. Everyone is always expected to be about making moves. It's like whenever you meet someone, the first question they ask you is "What do you do?" If you don't have an over the top answer for them, you start feeling like you're not doing enough. It's funny that when people ask us this question, we try to make our answer sound so good. We want to appear "worthy" to them, I guess. Although it is not always the case, we are accustomed to being judged based on what we do.

The amount of respect someone gives you, is often determined by your profession. For instance, when you tell someone you work at a fast food restaurant, they probably won't be wowed. They wouldn't feel like they needed to impress you in any way. However, if you tell someone that you're a movie producer, I'm pretty sure they'd be more interested in trying to connect with you on some level. They would go a bit more out of their way to acknowledge and respect you. I've seen it happen many times. However, what we should remember is that we will always meet people at different phases in their lives. The movie producer may have been a McDonalds employee a few years, or even a few days, before you met him. The person working at Chick-fil-A could be building a multi-million-dollar business on the side, while the movie producer could get fired the week after you meet him. Regardless, neither should be judged based on what they do to make a living. You never know what someone is doing behind the scenes. You could miss your biggest blessing, by focusing too much on the seen rather than the unseen.

Everyone deserves the same respect, regardless of what they do. Who ever said that grinding was the only way to achieve success? You can be doing a lot and nothing at all. A preacher named Tim Ross puts it like this, "You can be making moves and producing no fruit." He also says, "A lot of people want to look like they're doing something so bad, but why give up what you were created to do to look like you're doing something?" We need to stop getting so caught up in "the grind."

Instead, let's talk about doing the complete opposite of grinding. Michael Todd uses the word, stride instead of grind. What does striding actually mean? To stride means to walk with long, decisive steps in a specified direction. There may and probably will come a time in your life where striding will be very necessary. You may need to stride, if you're doing too many things at once and having a hard time hearing God. Maybe you need to stride, if you're doing a bunch of things but are unclear or maybe just a little bit unsure of where you're headed. For me, this was the case. I'm a person who is always on the move. I like to keep myself occupied. There came a time in my life, in 2018, when I was just moving, moving, moving. I was juggling school full-time (six classes), working almost 70 hours a week, traveling, hanging out and keeping up a social life (not even sure how that was possible). I was working on starting a blog and trying to write a book. I was doing all of this, but honestly, most of the truly important things in my life weren't in order, so my grind was pointless.

My financial situation was horrible, my relationship with God was pretty much dead and work and school were draining the life out of me. In July of 2018, I joined my current church, Change Church. That's when I realized how much I wasn't letting God lead my life. I've always had a major problem with hearing God. I used to always ask questions in church about hearing God, because I wanted to be ready for the experience when it presented itself. I always thought that when God spoke, it would be a very dramatic experience, like the heaven gates opening and him coming down sitting on my bed with an extreme deep voice saying, "JALIA!" Throughout my life, I looked for this kind of experience. When I never got it, I assumed He never spoke to me. Then I realized it wasn't how He speaks. He'll speak through books, people, circumstances, prayer, and His word. Most importantly, He'll speak directly to you. At that point in my life, I really needed Him to speak to me. I would literally pray about him speaking to me and wait, wait, wait. One day, I came across Michael Todd's series entitled, *Stride*. Finally, I found my answer! I knew why God was not speaking to me.

I WAS TOO BUSY FOR HIM.

I had so much going on in my life that I never put him into the equation. How could He speak to me, when I wasn't even making time to hear Him? If you're in a relationship and you express to your partner that you would like for them to communicate with you more, but you don't make the time for them to do so, how would it be possible? In this way, our relationship with God is like any other relationship we have. It requires effort. Todd says that God is a gentleman. He will knock at your door, but if you don't let him in, he will not kick the door down. God had been knocking at my door but I was not letting Him in. This is when I realized I was doing too much. I needed to take several seats. I knew, without doubt, that I needed to stop grinding and start striding. I cut back my work hours, held off on starting my book, hung out less, took some time off from traveling and just really took time to seek God.

During my sabbatical, I saw a major change in my life. My relationship with God grew and I got to church. Those were the two things that I had wanted for a long time. There were many other things that came into order during that time too, including my finances. As I sit here and write this book, I am nowhere near having everything all together. This book is being written during my process but I have made significant improvements, since I decided to shift from grinding to striding.

Even though striding is necessary, there are definitely challenges that you'll run into. Here are three of the challenges I ran into while learning to stride:

1.FOMO

FOMO is the Fear of Missing Out. I really thought that by stepping back from things, it would make me miss out on opportunities, people, experiences, etc. During my striding season, there were things and people that I needed to say no to. I was in a place where I needed to stay committed to certain things and anything outside of that, had to be turned down. Thankfully, during this time, God confirmed that I'd never miss out on what He has for me, as long as I'm doing what I am supposed to be doing. This is also true for you. As my pastor, Dr. Dharius Daniels says, "When it is your turn, God will move mountains and He will break down walls to get to you. He will part seas to make things happen for you."

This makes me think of the story in 1 Samuel Chapter 16. David, who was the son of Jesse, was minding his business tending the sheep. Samuel told Jesse there was a king there and he was introduced to all of Jesse's son's, besides David. Samuel told Jesse that the Lord had not chosen any of the sons he introduced him to and asked if there was another son. Jesse told him about David. Samuel said, "Send for him, for we will not sit down to eat until he arrives." God stopped what was going on, until David arrived. Meanwhile, David was minding his business. When God wants to call you or get your attention, He will make everyone stop until you arrive. You don't have to worry about being seen or getting noticed. People will see you, even when you think they don't. Don't let your striding season give you FOMO. You never have to fear missing out. As long as you stay connected with God, you'll stay covered and, in God's perfect timing, you'll be sent for and celebrated.

2. COMPARING

I mentioned this before, but it is absolutely worth repeating As a matter of fact, this just may have been the biggest challenge for me in my striding season. It is still a challenge for me now — the curse of comparing!

Scrolling on social media, seeing people doing this and that, just threw me for a loop. Constantly watching what other people were doing made me feel like I had to be doing something too. I felt that if I wasn't doing anything, I wasn't worthy or important. Dealing with comparison will have you asking yourself all types of questions. It really makes you genuinely believe that the next person's life is a million times better than yours. I really don't believe that the feelings which overwhelm us when we compare ourselves to others is jealousy. It is more of a reaction that triggers our competitive nature and makes us feel the social pressure of keeping up with others.

For we dare not class ourselves or compare ourselves
with those who commend themselves. But they,
measuring themselves by themselves, and comparing
themselves among themselves, are not wise.

2 CORINTHIANS 10:12 (NKJV)

3. THE DEADLINE BATTLE

Last of all, there's the good ole "deadline battle," also known as the fear of running out of time. Just like a teacher who sets deadlines, we're all known to have certain goals that we want to achieve by certain stages in our lives. If you would have spoken with the ten-year-old Jalia, by the age of twenty-six (the age I am right now), I would be married, living in a mansion with my husband and kids and working a beautiful career. I am twenty-six. Yet the deadline for having all of that done was by age twenty-five.

Now that I'm older, I still set deadlines. I still naively think I'm running out of time. It is as if I don't have more than half of my life still ahead of me. We all have deadlines set, but God does not go by our timelines. He goes by His. During my striding season, I needed to get over "The Deadline Battle." I needed to stop feeling like I was running out of time. Now don't get me wrong, when God says move, MOVE. Just don't mistake your striding season for a season of laziness or loss. It's not.

Several of the things I did during my striding season positively impacted my life. I know that you will greatly benefit from these four:

GOT INTO THE WORD

For the first time in my life, I started reading the Bible straight through. I would usually read pieces of scripture, small verses, or would just glance through. I never realized how alive the Bible really is, until I spent time in it. I never knew that the many questions that I had daily, would get answered once I opened the word of God the way I did during my striding season. Each book of the Bible is literally a different story. As a matter of fact, I could see myself in almost every book.

My advice to you during your striding season is to dive deep into the word of God. To be real, as good as it is, the Bible is a very difficult book to read. There are also many long and boring parts in it. To help you read through the Bible, a resource I suggest is *The 90-day Bible Challenge*, by Shaun Saunders on the podcast app. It helps you to read twelve pages a day for ninety days. He reads through the twelve pages and at the end of the reading, he thoroughly explains what he just read. This is a great resource, especially if you want a reading partner. Using the app definitely helped me.

You should also find a group of friends or family members who would want to read with you. This helps a lot. Although I am not completely through the entire Bible yet, what I have read so far, has changed my life.

STEWARDED EVERYTHING I HAD

There were many times in my striding season, when I just could not resist wanting more. I wanted more money, opportunities, resources and more everything. I was so focused on wanting more, that I forgot to focus on what I already had. We steadily ask God for more that we sometimes don't realize it. He is not going to give us more, until we learn how to steward what we currently have. Imagine being a supervisor on a job with specific duties and tasks. If handling your duties is already a struggle, would you ask your boss for more? No. You would try to get better at handling what you already had, before you ask for more to be added to your plate. This is what I had to learn to do. I had to learn to be a better steward of what I already had. Instead of asking God for more money, I learned how to better manage the money that I already had. Instead of asking for more opportunity, I learned how to better manage the current time I had. This is because once I received more opportunities, it would further limit my time. I focused on being a good steward over my little apartment, until I'm blessed with a house. I'm telling you, steward what you currently have before you ask God for more. God knows exactly how and when to give you more. You just have to trust Him.

SAT IN INTENTIONALITY

One of the most important things I made sure of during my striding time, was that I was intentional. What is intentionality? Intentionality is the act of being deliberate or purposeful. Everything that you do during your striding season should be done with intention. Don't do things haphazardly. Do things that are essential to your purpose. I am still taking action intentionally. I'm not totally clear on my next move, but every move I make now is done with intentionality.

PREPARED FOR THE NEXT STEP

Even though I'm not one hundred percent clear on my next step, I can prepare for it. That may sound confusing but hear me out. Before waiting for God's next instruction, do the last thing He told you to do and do it well. I heard someone say, "Purpose isn't a destination, it's a journey." Therefore, embrace the current journey you're on and eventually you'll realize that you are walking in your purpose. I used to think I had to find my purpose, but now I know it will be revealed to me. Make sure you're prepared for the next season that God has for you.

Striding

LET'S REFLECT
DAY#8

We all know that we live in a "grinding" kind of world. Everything is all about the grind. We're expected to grind day in and day out. If the next person isn't "grinding", they're considered to not be doing something right. Grinding became so normal, that anything else seems out of range. Everything is always expected to be about making moves.

Come to me, all you who are weary and burdened,
and I will give you rest.

MATTHEW 11:28

REFLECTION QUESTIONS

1. Are you striving or striding? In what ways are you doing this? It could be striving for the next best thing, striving to make a bunch of money, etc. Be honest with yourself.

____

____

____

____

2. What do you fear about striding? If you are in a striving season and need to enter into a striding season, what are some things you need to do in order to change?

____

____

____

____

Chapter 9

FIND A MENTOR

Having a mentor never really seemed important to me. I never put too much thought into it. One day my friend asked me how I felt about having a mentor. I told her that I didn't really care to have one. I figured, "I have friends for advice. What would I need a mentor for?" I was just ignorant about the whole mentor thing. Nonetheless, there are times when you just don't know what you need, until you get it. Obviously, you cann*ot know* that you need something or someone in your life, until they end up in your life. This was the case for me. The mentor I never knew I needed, was a gift from God. Her name is Elizabeth Pettus.

When I started my current job, I had the pleasure of meeting Elizabeth. She was the first colleague I met. We worked on an overnight shift together and got to know each other very well. We shared different parts of our lives and started to learn from one another. Aside from being a co-worker, I started to see Elizabeth as my friend. Eventually, I started to see our friendship as something even more. When we would converse, she would give me advice without me even asking for it. When I came to her with certain situations and scenarios, she would tell me things that I didn't want to hear but knew I needed to hear. Liz brought out many different parts of me. As a result, I started looking at myself through several different lenses. Without me even realizing it, she was guiding me. One day, Liz and I were having a serious conversation. She said, "Even though you never formally asked me to be, I am your mentor." I was so happy to hear her say that. Before then, I couldn't pinpoint what made our friendship different, but that was it. From that moment on, I knew how important it is to have a mentor.

Having a mentor is very important. They see vision that you do not see.

Elizabeth Pettus, Thank you.

Find a Mentor

LET'S REFLECT
DAY #9

Having a mentor is very important. They possess vision that you do not have.

> *Give instruction to a wise man, and he will be still*
> *wiser; teach a righteous man,*
> *and he will increase in learning.*

PROVERBS 9:9

REFLECTION QUESTIONS

1. Evaluate the characteristics that you believe that you would not only like, but NEED, in a mentor.

____

____

____

____

2. Write a list of at least five people by whom you could see yourself being mentored.

____

____

____

____

Chapter 10

BE INTENTIONAL

What does intentionality mean to you? I define intentionality as the sole purpose behind an act or thought, whether that thought is good or bad. The key word is *intention*. People either have good intentions or they have bad intentions. There are intentions behind every act. Whether those intentions are clear or unclear, is another thing. However, behind every action, there is some sort of intention.

Practicing having positive intentions is like giving yourself a gift. Being intentional about the way you live, the way you speak and the way you listen, can cause powerful outcomes. Every single time you're intentional about something, you go into it with a purpose. Practice telling yourself, "No matter how this turns out, my intentions are pure."

Bad intentions are malicious. No matter what has happened to you, if you go into something to purposely cause harm to someone or something, you will only end up hurting yourself. You may believe that only good intentions are planned.

Unfortunately, bad intentions are also planned. As I said, being very intentional with your life will always result in better outcomes. Some of the most significant areas in your life in which you want to be intentional are:

WHAT YOU SAY

Be very intentional with your words. Don't just be intentional about what you say, be intentional about how you say it. Your tone and facial expressions, as well as where and when you say what you need to say, all matter. All of these factors are very important, when you want to communicate effectively. I struggled with having a poor attitude for years. I was known to say whatever I wanted, whenever I wanted and however I wanted to say it. I wasn't mindful of who I was talking to. I justified myself, by saying they needed to hear the truth and they needed it raw. However, this attitude didn't evolve overnight. I developed that posture to protect myself. After years of being walked all over, I got fed up and started telling people off. I didn't always feel like I could speak up for myself. However, I learned that, in some ways, having a bad attitude protected me.

During my striding season, this is one of the traits that I spent time working on. I've learned that no matter what, you cannot talk to everyone the same way. You can't just "this is just how I am" everyone in your life. I learned to become very intentional with my words, not only for the other person but for myself. The old saying, "If you don't have anything nice to say, don't say anything at all," really does come in handy. I know this sounds silly, but it is a smart philosophy to live by.

You should be intentional with how you speak, because you don't want what you say to come across the wrong way. There are times when the person we are talking to can misconstrue our words. It's not always the other person's fault for mixing up our words. Sometimes, it's just how we communicated what we wanted to say. You should also be intentional with what you speak about because you never know who is listening to you. There are times when we can be talking and not know that a certain person is listening. This can be very true with children. Children listen to everything. They pick up on all of your words. This is a perfect example. Adults can be like children too. They also pick up on what you say. The last reason you should be intentional with what you say, is because, as the scriptures remind us, life and death is in the power of the tongue. Whether you believe it or not, you have the ability to speak things into your life, good and bad. You can speak things right into existence. Therefore, it's very important to be intentional with your words.

Death and life are in the power of the tongue: and
they that love it shall eat the fruit thereof.

PROVERBS 18:21

2. WHAT YOU LISTEN TO

We all know that we live in a day and age, in which social media is booming. There are so many different influencers online. Whether they are YouTubers, bloggers, pastors, actors, mentors, speakers, authors, musical artists, or something else, we have a plethora of social media content to listen to. Online and offline, we come across many people every day who are all speaking into us. This fact requires us to be very intentional about who and what we choose to listen to. Remember the old saying, "Everything that glitters ain't gold?" This is extremely relevant, when it comes to social media. This is because it promotes beautiful images of people who are not who they claim to be, despite how very convincing they appear to be. Everything looks good on social media. However, just because something looks right, doesn't mean that it is right. Be intentional about who and what you listening to.

3. THE WAY YOU REACT

This is probably the hardest one of them all. Reactions can be very difficult to control. We all know that you cannot control what others do to you. All you can control are your reactions. Learning to have an intentional reaction can be hard but is necessary. When someone hurts you, it can be a natural reaction to want to hurt them back. When someone provokes you, you're going to want to retaliate. Nonetheless, we have to come to terms with remembering that just because you want to do something, doesn't mean that you should. I think one of the most common areas we struggle with, is how we react at work. People at work will really try you the most, if you know what I mean. It is very hard, but important, not to react unintentionally at the workplace. Before you react, THINK.

Be Intentional

LET'S REFLECT
DAY #10

Every time you're intentional about something, you go into it with a purpose. You're telling yourself that no matter how this turns out, "my intentions were pure".

And the Lord answered me: "Write the vision; make
it plain on tablets, so he may run who reads it. For
still the vision awaits its appointed time; it hastens
to the end — it will not lie. If it seems slow, wait for it;
it will surely come; it will not delay

HABAKKUK 2:2-3

REFLECTION QUESTIONS

1. In what areas do you believe that you need to be a little more intentional?

____

____

____

____

2. God says, "Write the vision and make it plain." What is your vision?

____

____

____

____

Chapter 11

SEEK PURPOSE

Are you living or are you just alive? Are you seeking after your true purpose or just settling for mediocrity? Is what you're doing, helping build God's kingdom or is it just making you money?

There are many questions that can be asked pertaining to purpose. One thing is certain. Becoming your best self is a serious journey that we should all take. It can be very scary trying to live out our purpose in life. Sometimes we try so long to realize our purpose in life, that we start to get discouraged and then get comfortable where we are. We start to think that we have come as far as we are going to go. Therefore, we settle into believing that our current situation is all that God has called us to.

They say that the cemetery is one of the richest places in the world, because it is filled with so much untapped potential. Why is this? It is because people do not live out their purpose in life. It is almost as if we don't want to become all that God wants us to be. We really do have the ability to become all that we can be, but we often just have many roadblocks, excuses, and unexpected experiences that hold us back. As a result, we fail to push through and fulfill God's plan for our lives.

As I have emphasized throughout this book, things like losing ourselves, failure, struggling to let go, mistakes, insecurities, rough pasts, relationships, depression and loneliness are major roadblocks that can hold us back. It is definitely not easy to overcome trauma, pain, anger, disappointment and loss. However, with God you can bounce back from any situation. We have to quit letting these situations define us and keep us from staying on the path that God has for us.

I believe that to become all that you can be, there are a few things which must be adjusted. Once you make the adjustment, you will get to where you are destined to be:

ADJUST YOUR LEAN

God wants you to be close with him. Sometimes we need to sit back and adjust who we choose to lean on. God should truly be at the top of your pyramid. He wants to be included in every area of our lives. This means that we have to build a strong relationship with him daily. There is nothing you can do without Him. I mean absolutely nothing. Anything you try to do on your own, will always backfire if it is not what He wants for you. Like I said before, God has a plan for you and His plans are way better than your own. You have to understand that there can and will be times when you are working on something for a long time. It is tricky because working on something for a long time can have you believing that God has called you to that thing. However, sometimes that work really isn't God ordained. This is why we have to prepare ourselves. We have to be able to discern when something isn't for us, even if it feels like it is. In order to be able to hear God, you have to be available to listen to Him and hear Him. Sometimes that means that you have to step back from some things and some people and just spend as much time with God as possible. It means that you have to yearn for His voice. Ask Him questions, tell Him your plans, include Him in all areas of your life and just let Him know that you want Him to have full control.

This year has been a very quiet year for me. I have been seeking God like never before. I am used to being everywhere and doing everything. However, God told me loud and clear to "slow down" and Michael Todd helped me realize how fast I'd been moving with his series called, *Stride*. Instead of striving to do things all the time, we should focus more on striding. Striding means to take long decisive steps in a specific direction. By now, you guys know that I am a planner. I want to plan everything. Hence the title of this book "I didn't plan for this." However, not this year. God sat me still and built me up. He knows that I am not quite ready for what He has in store for me. This may also be the case for you. I just need you to know that during your time of waiting, be patient. This is the time to really lean on Him, seek Him and know Him. Prepare to become your best self, because your time is coming. He is testing you while you wait. Do not be discouraged.

> *Trust in the Lord with all your heart and lean not on your own understanding; in all your ways submit to him, and he will make your paths straight.*

PROVERBS 3:5-6

2. ADJUST YOUR LENSES

Do not confuse what you see for yourself, with what God sees for you. Many times our plans and his plans are not synonymous. You're praying for a job, but God wants you to be the CEO of your own company. You're praying to lose weight, but God wants you to just be healthy and comfortable in your body. You're praying for more money to pay your rent, but God is preparing you for an overflow, so that you can purchase an entire complex. Whatever you want for yourself, picture God wanting bigger and better. This is because He always sees and wants more for you than you do for yourself.

One very important thing that my pastor, Dharius Daniels, teaches, is that we must never tie dysfunction to who we are. Any dysfunction is not a part of who you are. A perfect example is how much of a procrastinator I can be. When I say, I am the world's best procrastinator, I mean it. If there were some kind of award for this trait; I would win it. I always believe that I do my best work at the last minute. Nonetheless, a procrastinator is not who I am. Procrastinating is a dysfunction that I sometimes exhibit. It is something that I do. However, in God's eyes, I am very productive and I can get things done early. God wants me to be the productive child He called me to be. I can believe, at times, that I am not good enough. However, in God's eyes, I am more than enough. We are all precious in God's eyes. I mean we are very precious. He died for us, and if you ask me, it does not get any better than that. If we get more in tuned, we will be able to see ourselves the way God sees us and we will begin to flourish and become all that we can be.

> *But you are his chosen people, the King's priests.*
> *You are a holy man, people who belong to God. He*
> *chose you to tell about the wonderful things he has*
> *done. He brought you out of the darkness of sin into*
> *his wonderful light.*

1 PETER 2:9

3. ADJUST YOUR LIFESTYLE

You may need a lifestyle adjustment. Stop focusing so much on other people and on other things. Learn to start investing in yourself.

I can't even begin to express how important it is to invest in yourself. When you're investing in yourself, you are choosing yourself. You are putting yourself first. This means that you stop making excuses and waiting for things to happen. Instead, you take concrete actions that will allow you to win. The only one you should ever wait on is God. Once God gives you a clear, distinct yes, never backtrack and don't stand still. Go as far as you can go. Just make sure you go with God.

Here are twelve amazing ways to invest in yourself:

1. Pray daily
2. Read scriptures, books, blogs, articles and magazines

3. Be teachable in every situation
4. Create multiple streams of incomes
5. Get a mentor
6. Practice daily affirmations
7. Perfect your craft
8. Create a wall full of positive things about yourself
9. Allow room in your life for new blessings
10. Keep distractions from hindering your progress
11. Don't be afraid to step outside of your comfort zone
12. SERVE OTHERS!

4. ADJUST YOUR LINEUP

Everyone cannot go where you are going. It doesn't matter how long you've known someone or how close you are, some people just aren't meant to be on certain parts of your journey. That is completely okay. You have to know when it is time to adjust your lineup, so that you can add and delete people in and out of your life, as needed. Don't be afraid to let people go. Don't get too attached. Don't let familiarity mess up what God has planned for you. In order to become all that you can be, you must divorce comfort. Things and people in your life will change at certain times in your life. Do not stop evolving because of this. Keep going. Keep building yourself. Take an inventory of everyone in your life. This will help you to understand who should be there and who shouldn't. Love everyone and learn from everyone, but do not walk closely with everyone.

As iron sharpens iron, so a friend sharpens a friend.

PROVERBS 27:17

Walk with the wise and become wise; associate with fools and get in trouble.

PROVERBS 13:20

Seek Purpose

LET'S REFLECT
DAY #11

Are you living or just alive? Are you seeking after your true purpose or just settling for mediocrity? Is what you're doing helping build God's kingdom or is it just making you money? There are many questions that can be asked pertaining to purpose. Becoming your best self is a serious journey that we should all be headed towards. It can be scary how most of us can be living out of our purpose sometimes for so long, that we start to just get comfortable being there. We start thinking that our current situation is all that God has called us to. They say that the cemetery is filled with so much potential. However, why is this? It is because people do not live out their purpose. It's almost like we don't want to become all that God wants us to be.

Many are the plans in a person's heart, but it is the LORD's purpose that prevails.

PROVERBS 19:21

REFLECTION QUESTIONS

1. What does purpose mean to you? How do you describe it? There are many definitions and points of view on purpose. However, what is your clear-cut definition and view of it?

____

____

____

____

2. What can you do to make sure that you are living an "on purpose" kind of life?

____

____

____

Chapter 12

COME BACK TO CHRIST

I WAS LOST

I was so far from where I was supposed to be. I gave up on church. I gave up on church people. I almost even gave up on God. I started to say things like, "I don't need to be in church to love God," and "God knows my heart." I even questioned at times, if He was real. These were things that I was saying out of hurt and frustration. I was running. Many thoughts that ran through my head, but I just kept rebelling. I ended up so far from God, that I could honestly feel His absence in my soul. I could literally feel the distance, but something inside me still knew that I needed Him. Just like a lost child who ran away from her parents, I wanted to find my way back home. So, what did I do? I called out for God. I felt abandoned. I knew I needed to feel God's love, but unfortunately at that time, I just could not feel it. It was like a quiet, but very rough storm. I didn't know what was going to happen, but then God stepped in.

I HAD TO REPENT

Before I did anything else, I knew I had to repent. The way I was living was not God's way. I needed to have a conversation with him about it.

This passage of scripture really spoke to me during my time of repentance,

> *It's true that God is all-powerful, but he doesn't bully innocent people. For the wicked, though, it's a different story — he doesn't give them the time of day but champions the rights of their victims. He never takes his eyes off the righteous; he honors them lavishly, promotes them endlessly. When things go badly, when affliction and suffering descend, God tells them where they've gone wrong, shows them how their pride has caused their trouble. He forces them to heed his warning, tells them they must repent of their bad life. If they obey and serve him, they'll have a good, long life on easy street. But if they disobey, they'll be cut down in their prime and never know the first thing about life. Angry people without God pile grievance upon grievance, always blaming others for their troubles. Living it up in sexual excesses, virility wasted, they die young. But those who learn from their suffering, God delivers from their suffering.*

JOB 36:7 (MSG)

Repenting to God can be really hard. This is especially true when you know you've been living a life that does not please Him at all.

WHAT IS REPENTANCE?

Most of the definitions in the dictionary about repentance talk about regret. I am not really feeling that definition because some of my most valuable lessons have come through my repentance. I'm not saying make mistakes just to repent. I am saying that repentance can be a remarkable experience, especially when it is done authentically. Repentance is all about transparency. It is not God's job to ask you to tell Him what you did wrong, it is your job to bring it to Him.

HOW TO REPENT

1. RECOGNIZE YOUR SIN

The first step to repentance is recognition. It can and will be really hard to repent to God, without taking a step back and realizing where you actually missed the mark. You have to know where you are, not just physically, but also emotionally and spiritually. You have to know where you are, so that you can know exactly what to bring to Him. Be honest with yourself, because God can only truly help you and meet you where you are, when you are honest.

This brings me to a very popular story in the Bible, which is found in Genesis Chapter three. There we meet Adam and Eve in the Garden of Eden right after they shamefully tried to cover themselves with fig leaves, after they had sinned by eating from the tree that God told them not to touch. Now I need you to pay close attention to this passage, since it lines up with what I am trying to tell you:

> *God called to the Man: "Where are you?" He said, "I heard you in the garden and I was afraid because I was naked. And I hid." God said, "Who told you you were naked? Did you eat from that tree I told you not to eat from?"*
>
> GENESIS 3:9-11

First and foremost, the question, "Where are you?" is powerful in itself. Don't look over it because it sounds simple. God knew exactly where they were. It wasn't really a question that He needed an answer to. He was trying to see if *they* knew where they were. I think He was also trying to see if they were going to tell the truth. The next two verses are an indication that they truly recognized where they went wrong and how. Knowing where you went wrong and how you went wrong are very important. However, you can't just have your shortcomings in your head. Speak out loud when you talk to God. Yell if you have to.

In verse eleven, the question, "Who told you you were naked?" made me think about how we, at times, listen to the opinions and directions of others and believe what they tell us, even when what they say is not true. Sometimes we think repentance means going to God any time a person tells us we have done something wrong or not pleasing to God. My question is, Who do you believe? God or man?

116

2. Take a Reality Check

This is the hardest part of the process. This involves something most humans despise doing, which is to stop long enough to feel and then to be brave enough to sit with their reality. Have you ever experienced going through a difficult emotion and trying your best to force yourself to be numb to it? This happens a lot. It is our way of coping. It is also a way to deal with shame and embarrassment. Instead of sitting with and feeling the emotions or embracing the truth of how we feel, we walk or run from it.

Repentance is all about facing your reality and knowing that just because it is your reality at a given moment in time, does not mean that it will be your reality forever because God forgives you for it. He came to heal you from it. Sitting with your reality can also open the doors to you forgiving yourself and to being open enough to make yourself accountable, so that you can guard against falling in the future.

3. Surrender

What does it mean to surrender? It is basically handing over the control of something. Surrendering in repentance means giving God full access and entry into your situation. Remember that God is a gentleman. He will not stay where he is not wanted. He will not rush through areas of your life that you don't invite him into. Open your mouth and say to God, "I surrender all. I surrender my life to you."

This lets God know that you trust Him, and you want Him to take over. This was the most important part for me, when I was returning back to God. There were parts about myself that I just was not sure whether I wanted to invite Him into yet. However, I surrendered. I can now say that whatever you bring to God, He will turn it around, if you surrender.

3. READ YOUR BIBLE

As I shared, I started to dig deep into my Bible. The Bible literally came alive, once I started to read it. This discipline helped me to rebuild my relationship with God and seek Him more. The Bible cannot speak to you, unless you read it. You cannot read the Bible, unless you open it.

The Truth is that the Bible is, without a doubt, unlike any other book you will ever read. It will read you more than you read it. I never knew what people meant when they said that the Bible will speak to you and bring perspective, until I really dedicated myself to reading it. Although I was in church my entire life, I did not realize the power of reading the word of God, until I was twenty-six years old.

Crazy, right? I know. All of those years in church, "knowing God" and praying, yet I can honestly say that I'd never taken a serious dive into the Bible. Amazingly, when I started to read it, I realized all of the reasons why I had not done so before. Number one, it takes patience. It is not, of course, a short book to read. It can also be very difficult to read and sometimes, spending time trying to understand it can also take quite a while. There were times where I spent months trying to understand one passage.

Honestly, at times, it can also be very boring to read. Yes, I said it, it can be boring. For example, I found the book of Leviticus to be boring and slightly difficult to read.

118

The Bible can also be very repetitive. However, believe it or not, as I am getting deeper into the Bible, I understand more why books like Leviticus had to be written. The purpose of Leviticus was to provide the instructions and laws needed to guide a sinful, although redeemed, people in their relationship with God. Now, back to the boring part. Don't get me started with all of the names in the Bible. They are very difficult to pronounce. The parts that mention huge family lines can be very long and boring. However, if you can get through these parts of the Bible, I promise that you will reap the benefits and rewards of reading it. You just have to keep reading.

Reading the Bible needs to be considered a meal, rather than a chore. Nobody really likes the idea of a chore. It feels like you're forced. It feels like you have to do it, rather than like you want to do it. However, we enjoy our meals, don't we? Think of reading the Bible like mealtime. You're getting fed. You're eating, until you become full. You want to eat, because if you don't you will go hungry. Trust me, without the word of God, you will starve.

5. DEVELOP A PRAYER LIFE

I had to pray. You cannot have a relationship with God without spending time with Him in prayer. I always thought that when I prayed to God, I had to be in a specific place and use a specific tone of voice. Believing this caused me not to talk to Him as often as I should -- which is every day. My prayers were always more monologues than dialogues. I then started to realize that I can talk to God, just like I talk to some of my friends. Instead of "So, hey girl," I started saying "So, hey God." I started changing my prayers from vague prayers to specific prayers. Instead of saying "God protect me." I started saying things like, "God protect me on the road, while I am driving to work." I started to be very transparent with my prayers, so that God could freely bless and deliver me. Another thing I noticed about my prayer life, is that I put too much pressure on myself. I felt that if I didn't pray 23 ½ hours out of a 24-hour day, that my prayer life sucked. This obviously wasn't the case. You can talk to God all throughout your day or you can talk to Him all day. However, I think what is most important, is starting your day and ending your day with talking to God. All in all, He wants to be close to you, so talk to Him.

6. YEARN FOR GOD'S VOICE

I attended a conference years ago at which Donnie McClurkin was a speaker. There were many people at this conference, yet as I made my way to the altar, he came up to me and started to pray and prophesy over me. I'll never forget what he said to me. He told me that I needed to be ready, because God wanted to use me for my generation. I was very young at the time. It was around the time I first gave my life to Christ. He said that I needed to stop running, and let God use me. The crazy thing is, at the time, I wasn't running. However, years later, I found myself running as far away from God as I could run. Although it was many years later, that prophecy played over and over in my head during my return to God.

I am at a place now where I solely yearn for God's voice. I can truly say that God has started to speak to me, since I started to do the things I shared with you in this chapter. I know that with patience, I will be able to hear Him more clearly. However, for now, I will remain obedient and connected to Him.

120

I AM FREE

I can honestly say that I found freedom. Once God enters your life, you really cannot imagine your life without Him. He will come into your life and do a new thing. Living as a Christian does not mean that you won't experience bad things. It does mean that you won't have to experience them alone. When I returned to God, I instantly became more free. I was more free of fear, loneliness, pain, hurt and anxiety. I was more free of everything that goes against what He has predestined for my life.

I AM JALIA WALLACE AND I AM FREE!

Come Back to Christ

LET'S REFLECT
DAY #12

Someone who wants to quit smoking, an aspiring doctor and a baby learning how to walk all have one thing in common: having to take the next step to reach a goal. Even a baby has to take a step to learn to start walking. They usually struggle at first, because they don't want to fall. Therefore, they usually refuse to let go of their parent's hand. However, they'll never fully start walking, until they get the courage to take that first step. Just like a baby, I believe that we of struggle with taking the first step in our lives. We get afraid to let go of our comfort zone and familiarity, just like a baby is afraid to let go of their parent's hand. That is just what they are used to. What scares us the most? It can be several things. However, I'm going to argue that the main reasoning of why people fear taking the next step, is the fear of failing or falling.

"Come," he said. Then Peter got down out of the boat, walked on the water and came toward Jesus. 30 But when he saw the wind, he was afraid and, beginning

*to sink, cried out, "Lord, save me!" Immediately
Jesus reached out his hand and caught him. "You of
little faith," he said, "Why did you doubt?"*

MATTHEW 14: 29-31 29

REFLECTION QUESTIONS

1. What do you wish to be more free of?

____

____

____

____

2. Living with God does not mean that you will not experience bad things, but it does mean that you will not have to
   experience them alone. God will help you. Have you given
   your life to Christ yet?

____

____

____

____

Chapter 13

TAKE THE NEXT STEP

Someone who wants to quit smoking, an aspiring physician and a baby learning how to walk, all have one thing in common. Each of them has to take the next step, in order to reach their goal. Even a baby has to take a step to learn to start walking. They usually struggle at first, because they don't want to fall. As a result, they may refuse to let go of their parent's hand. However, they'll never fully start walking, until they get the courage to take that first step. Well, just like a baby who is learning to walk, we often struggle with taking the next step in our lives. We become afraid to let go and we cling to our comfort zones. What scares us the most? It can be several things. However, I'm going to argue that the main reasoning people fear taking the next step, is the fear of falling or failing.

Remember early in the book when I said there are things that we prepare for and things that we don't prepare for? We know by now that failing and falling are two things for which we are seldom prepared. None of us prepare to fail, but we will fail. Failure is not always a bad thing. In fact, most of the time it isn't. Failure is an indication that you actually had the courage to do something and that you did not let fear of the outcome hold you back.

I always loved to read as a kid. I started reading advanced books very young, so I guess you could say that I was smart. I remember loving to read Mary Kate and Ashley, The Babysitters Club, Harry Potter, and whatever else I could get my tiny hands on. I visited the library daily and had my own library card. I would always check out a few books at a time, because I would go through them very fast. Once I was done reading one book, I was more than ready for the next. I loved stories. I loved being able to feel the characters in the books. I felt like I was escaping reality, while I was reading. It was like I entered a whole different world when I read. I'm convinced that reading can be a form of therapy.

At that time, I never imagined that I would be sitting here writing my own book. I'm not even going to say, "I always knew I would write a book," because I didn't. As I got older, I thought about it here and there, but not enough to believe I would actually execute it. Even though I've been reading all my life and eager to tell a story and encourage others, it wasn't until the end of 2018, when I woke up with the craziest idea. The thought of writing a book just popped into my head. However, it wasn't just any thought, it was an "I have to do this!" kind of thought.

Of course, I had never written a book before, so I immediately became anxious and automatically started to doubt myself. I remember my pastor preaching a sermon on New Year's Eve entitled, "Level Up." If there was one thing I remembered from his message, it was when he said, "You need a heavy anointing, because you have a big assignment -- build anyway." Even though this is just the beginning of my journey, and there will be much more to come, I felt like this was my starting place.

I had a strong desire burning inside of me to get this message out. I know from experience, and just from looking around me, that people forget to work on themselves. We forget that aside from everything else, we have to prepare to become our best selves, if we are going to be ready for all we are destined for. I knew that it was going to require a lot of time, dedication, and consistency to write this book. However, I also knew that until I took that next step, I would forever be withholding my assignment.

I prayed about it and I waited until I got a good feeling about it. I then started to research all kinds of "writing your first book" websites and articles. I even went to a few book writing seminars, where different authors shared their journeys about book writing. As I continued to research, I realized just one thing. It was that the hardest part about any task is actually starting. No matter how much research I did, how many tips I came across and how many examples I looked at, I was never going to actually start until I started. Taking the first step is always the hardest, but I started with my outline and went from there.

This process can be applied to anything in life. Unfortunately, it still doesn't automatically get easier after taking the first step. The rest requires the consistency to follow through. Continue to build yourself or to rebuild yourself, if you have to. Remember that God has all of your steps planned. He had them planned before you were even born, so there's no point in even tripping. He already knows your whole story, while you're still waiting on certain chapters to be revealed. In the book, *Allowing God the Control*, author Warren Coleman speaks about taking your hand off of things and giving the control back to God. I pray and hope that you continue to trust the process. Trust the process. Trust the process.

We humans keep brainstorming options and plans,
but God's purpose prevails.

PROVERBS 19:21

By all means, be unapologetically you. Start today. Remember, you will run into many situations on your path fulfilling God's plan in your life, in which you holler, "I Didn't Plan for This!" When you do, just remember that everything will work out for you, because even when you didn't plan for the unexpected, trying test and trials of life, God did.

Take the Next Step

LET'S REFLECT
DAY #13

Once God enters your life, you really cannot imagine your life without him. He will come into your life and do a new thing. Living as a Christian does not mean that you won't experience the bad, but you won't have to experience it alone. When I returned to God, I just became freer. More free of fear, loneliness, pain, hurt, anxiety and everything that goes against what he has on and for my life.

And be not conformed to this world: but be ye transformed by the renewing of your mind, that ye may prove what [is] that good, and acceptable, and perfect, will of God

ROMANS 12:2

1. What blocks or makes you afraid of taking the steps necessary to do something new? The thing that has been heavy on your mind could turn out to be something great! Take the next step.

____

____

____

____

2. Where in your life is God asking you to have the faith of Peter who walked on water? What do you have a strong desire to do but are afraid to do?

____

____

____

____

About the Author

Jalia is the youngest in a family of five. She has two older sisters, Jasmin and Joanae. She has two nephews, one niece and one Godson. She was born in Philadelphia, PA but currently resides in Lindenwold, NJ. She is an active member at *Change Church,* where she serves under the amazingly strong leadership of Dr. Dharius Daniels and Lady Shameka Daniels.

Jalia earned an Associate's Degree in Business Administration in 2016. She is currently pursuing her bachelor's degree in Fashion Merchandising Management, with a concentration in Buying, at Philadelphia University, where she also studied abroad in China.

Jalia currently works as a direct support professional, where she cares for individuals of all ages with developmental disabilities. She has a strong passion for helping others and looks forward to furthering her career in ways that enable her to be of even greater service to her community.

Jalia can be described as resilient, creative, strategic, adventurous and charismatic. Her mission is to help people of all ages, especially youth and young adults, to be saved and to experience their true identity in Christ.

Salvation Prayer

Dear Jesus, I know that I am a sinner and have fallen short over and over again. I do believe that you died for my sins and rose again from the dead to wash away all of my sins. I want nothing more than to invite you into my life as my own personal savior and I want to walk alongside you. I know that this will not always be easy, but with you I know and trust that it will be worth it.

Love,
Your Child (Insert Your Name)

For whosoever shall call upon the name of the Lord shall be saved.

ROMANS 10:13